Berkshire and Oxfordshire

LES MAPLE

COUNTRYSIDE BOOKS
NEWBURY BERKSHIRE

First published 2005
© Les Maple, 2005

COUNTRYSIDE BOOKS
3 Catherine Road
Newbury, Berkshire

To view our complete range of books,
please visit us at
www.countrysidebooks.co.uk

ISBN 1 85306 897 7

Photographs by the author

Designed by Peter Davies, Nautilus Design
Produced through MRM Associates Ltd., Reading
Typeset by Techniset Typesetters, Newton-le-Willows
Printed by Woolnough Bookbinding Ltd., Irthlingborough

Contents

INTRODUCTION

WALKS IN BERKSHIRE

1.	**Upper Lambourn:** The Malt Shovel (7 miles)	7
2.	**Hungerford:** The Down Gate (6½ miles)	11
3.	**Inkpen Common:** The Crown and Garter (6¼ miles)	14
4.	**Chaddleworth:** The Ibex (5 miles)	17
5.	**Crockham Heath:** The Craven Arms (3¾ or 6½ miles)	20
6.	**Bagnor:** The Blackbird (6 miles)	23
7.	**West Ilsley:** The Harrow Inn (7 miles)	27
8.	**Hermitage:** The Fox Inn (5½ miles)	30
9.	**Aldworth:** The Bell Inn (4¾ or 6½ miles)	34
10.	**Aldermaston Wharf:** The Butt Inn (6 miles)	37
11.	**Pangbourne:** The Cross Keys (6 miles)	40
12.	**Swallowfield:** The George and Dragon (5 or 6¼ miles)	44
13.	**Finchampstead:** The Queen's Oak (7 miles)	48
14.	**Hurst and Dinton Pastures:** The Green Man (6 miles)	51
15.	**Crazies Hill:** The Horns (4½ miles)	55
16.	**Littlewick Green:** The Cricketers (6 miles)	58
17.	**Cookham Dean:** The Jolly Farmer (4½ miles)	62
18.	**Swinley Forest (Bracknell):** The Golden Retriever (5½ miles)	65
19.	**Woodside (Ascot):** The Rose and Crown (6 miles)	68
20.	**Old Windsor:** The Union Inn (6 miles)	71

Contents

WALKS IN OXFORDSHIRE

21. **Shenington:** The Bell Inn (3 or 5 miles) — 75
22. **North Newington:** The Blinking Owl Inn (5½ miles) — 78
23. **Salford and the Rollright Stones:** The Black Horse (7¼ miles) — 81
24. **Clifton (Deddington):** The Duke of Cumberland's Head (5¼ miles) — 85
25. **Fringford:** The Butchers Arms (6¼ miles) — 88
26. **Lower Heyford:** The Bell Inn (5 miles) — 92
27. **Shipton-under-Wychwood:** The Shaven Crown Hotel (6¾ miles) — 95
28. **Combe:** The Cock Inn (5½ miles) — 99
29. **Stanton St John:** The Star Inn (5½ miles) — 103
30. **Alvescot:** The Plough Inn (5¾ miles) — 107
31. **Cuddesdon:** The Bat and Ball Inn (4 miles) — 110
32. **Sydenham:** The Crown Inn (6¼ miles) — 113
33. **Longworth:** The Blue Boar (5½ miles) — 117
34. **Coleshill:** The Radnor Arms (6 miles) — 120
35. **Sutton Courtenay:** The Swan (6¼ miles) — 124
36. **Watlington:** The Carriers Arms (6 miles) — 128
37. **Uffington:** The Fox and Hounds (6 miles) — 131
38. **East Hendred:** The Plough Inn (6 miles) — 134
39. **Satwell:** The Lamb Inn (5½ miles) — 137
40. **Shiplake Row:** The White Hart (6½ miles) — 141

PUBLISHER'S NOTE

We hope that you obtain considerable enjoyment from this book; great care has been taken in its preparation. Although at the time of publication all routes followed public rights of way or permitted paths, diversion orders can be made and permissions withdrawn.

We cannot, of course, be held responsible for such diversion orders and any inaccuracies in the text which result from these or any other changes to the routes nor any damage which might result from walkers trespassing on private property. We are anxious though that all details covering the walks are kept up to date and would therefore welcome information from readers which would be relevant to future editions.

However, for the benefit of a proper map, we do recommend that you purchase the relevant Ordnance Survey sheet covering your walk. The Ordnance Survey maps are widely available, especially through booksellers and local newsagents.

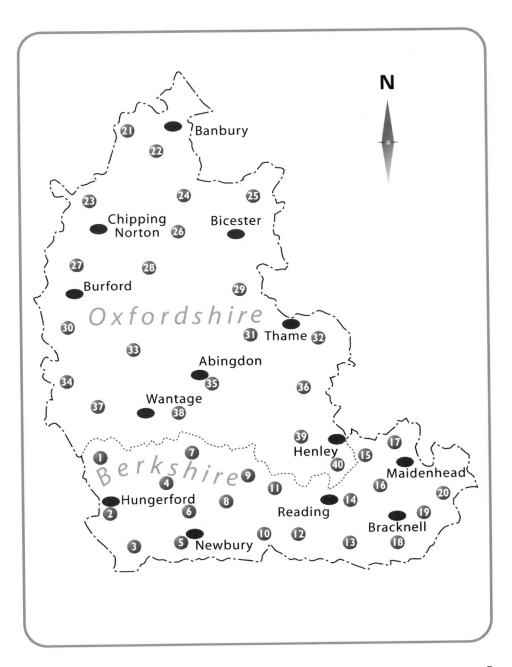

N

Banbury

Chipping
Norton

Bicester

Burford

Oxfordshire

Thame

Abingdon

Wantage

Henley

Maidenhead

Berkshire

Hungerford

Reading

Bracknell

Newbury

Introduction

A pleasant drive, an interesting walk, a friendly pub providing good food, and the possibility of visiting a place of interest nearby – these make an ideal combination for spending a leisurely day in the countryside. The 40 circular walks in this book provide an opportunity to do just that. Starting and finishing at, or near to, a recommended pub or inn, each route takes you through some of the attractive, and contrasting, scenery that Berkshire and Oxfordshire have to offer.

The walks in Berkshire provide an opportunity to relive some of the county's long and varied history. Visit the sites of Iron Age hill forts and Neolithic barrows. View English Civil War sites at Wash Common and at Donnington, both on the outskirts of Newbury. Learn about the history of the Kennet and Avon Canal. Walk along sections of the Ridgeway, the oldest thoroughfare in the country, which runs through both Berkshire and Oxfordshire. Take in stretches of the tranquil River Thames and other smaller rivers and streams. Visit interesting towns and pretty villages, with their churches, thatched cottages, pubs, coaching inns, and literary connections. Walk through woodland that once formed part of a great forest covering most of Berkshire, or in Windsor Great Park or even across Ascot Racecourse.

Oxfordshire, located in the heart of England, has a great diversity of scenery, heritage, attractive villages and historic towns. The county is a gem of hidden delights and is well worth investigating on foot. The landscape encompasses the plains and valleys of the River Thames and its tributaries, the Thame, Cherwell, Evenlode and Windrush; the rolling hills and dry-stone walls of the Cotswolds; the ironstone of north Oxfordshire; the steep slopes and wooded hills of the Chilterns; and the historic Vale of the White Horse, which until 1974 was part of Berkshire. It is a landscape that, together with its many picturesque villages, has inspired musicians, poets and artists to capture it in their own individual style. Witness the magic of the mysterious Rollright Stones; wonder at the remains of the Roman villa at North Leigh; take time out to visit Blenheim Palace, England's largest country house and birthplace of Winston Churchill. Discover interesting inns, churches and parkland; walk sections of Oxfordshire's long distance paths: the Ridgeway, the Thames Path, Oxfordshire Way, Macmillan Way, the Oxford Canal and the D'Arcy Dalton Way. This is rural England at its very best.

Each route is between 3 and 7¼ miles in length. You will usually be able to park at the pub whilst doing the walk so long as you intend to call in for some refreshment. However, it is only courteous to ask the landlord before setting out. Very few of the walks are accessible by public transport, although some of the circuits do start within a few miles of some of the major towns in both counties. A sketch map, indicating the route to be followed, accompanies each of the walks. However, it is strongly recommended that you carry the relevant OS map with you for more detailed information.

On your expeditions it is advisable that you carry waterproofs, a snack and most importantly a drink, especially on hot days. At the end of the circuit, please ensure that you change your footwear and leave any muddy boots in the car before entering the pub.

Les Maple

The Malt Shovel

border, which it follows as it ascends the Downs. From the top there are some excellent views looking back towards Wiltshire in the west and towards Oxfordshire in the north. Passing a number of racehorse training gallops, the route follows the Lambourn Valley Way back to the village.

Upper Lambourn, situated close to the Wiltshire and Oxfordshire borders, lies in a remote part of the Berkshire Downs. Leaving the village the route heads towards the Oxfordshire

Distance: 7 miles

OS Explorer 170 Abingdon, Wantage & Vale of White Horse, with just the starting point on 158 Newbury & Hungerford GR 318799

An undulating walk with some gradual ascents and descents

Starting point: The Malt Shovel. Please obtain permission to leave your car in the car park while you are walking. There are some spaces available elsewhere in the village.

How to get there: Upper Lambourn is situated just off the B4000, ½ mile north-west of Lambourn. From the B4000, turn into Maltshovel Lane. The inn is on the left at the far end of the lane.

The **Malt Shovel** is thought to be over 350 years old. Situated deep in the heart of horse racing countryside some of its regular customers may include trainers, jockeys and stable lads. On the walls of the lounge and public bars are various photographs of racing scenes. There is a small garden just across the road from the pub. Children and dogs are welcome. Beers available include Fuller's London Pride, John Smith's and 1744 lager. Typical bar food, such as sandwiches, baguettes and chips, is available at lunchtimes, and pizzas in the evening.

Opening times are 11 am to 11 pm on Monday to Saturday and 12 noon to 10.30 pm on Sunday. Food is available from 12 noon to 2 pm and 7 pm to 9.30 pm. This could change and it is advisable to ring if possible.

Telephone: 01488 71623.

7

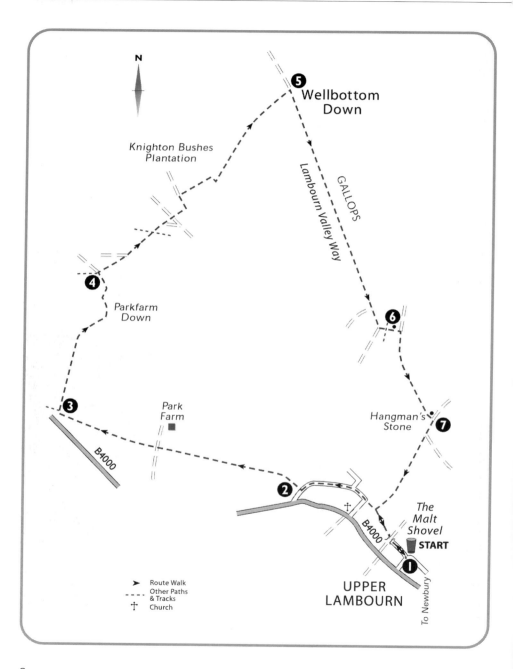

UPPER
LAMBOURN

Legend:
➤ Route Walk
--- Other Paths & Tracks
† Church

The Walk

1 Leaving the inn car park, turn left and, at the road junction, left again. Note the thatched cottage you pass on the left. It has a sign that states that it is 'of special historic and architectural interest'. Where the road bends right, continue straight ahead along the Fulke Walwyn Way. The path runs alongside a ditch. When this ends, continue straight ahead along the road, ignoring both a turning on the right and another on the left. Follow the road round a wide left-hand bend to reach a bridleway on the right, just past a thatched cottage.

2 Turn right along a metalled drive. Where this ends, at Frenchman's House, continue straight ahead on a grassy track.

Fields soon open out on either side. At Park Farm the track becomes metalled again. Where this bends left carry straight on along the farm track, with a fence on each side. The undulating countryside of the Berkshire Downs is clearly visible all around. To your left, the B4000 runs almost parallel to the track. Ahead, and slightly to your left, on the other side of the road lies Ashdown House, sadly hidden by surrounding woodland.

3 On reaching a T-junction, turn right uphill. The left-hand side of the track, at this point, runs along the Oxfordshire border. Ignore a stile on the left and continue to ascend gradually as the track bends right then left over Parkfarm Down. You eventually arrive at a junction. A path veers off to the left and

Racehorses heading out for the downs.

9

there are some large rocks and a wooden post on the right.

4 At this junction, turn right downhill. Where a track joins from the left, continue straight ahead. Maintain direction over a cross track (byway) and keep on the track as it bends left towards a corner of Knighton Bushes Plantation. Turn right here, keeping the plantation on your left. At the far end the track bends right, then left. A long, gradual ascent now follows up to Wellbottom Down. At the top you reach a five bar gate and a cross track – the Lambourn Valley Way.

5 Turn right along the Lambourn Valley Way. The possibility of seeing racehorses going through their paces is quite high along here as the track passes between training gallops. Down in the valley to your left, near a clump of trees, are the Seven Barrows ancient burial mounds, which are thought to date back to the Bronze Age. The barrows are not clearly visible from this distance. Continue along the main track until you reach a hedge on the left. At a T-junction, just after the hedge ends, turn left between barrier fences. Go over a racehorse crossing point and head towards a barn.

6 Pass to the right of the barn and go down a slope to reach a cross track. Turn right here and at the first junction fork left. Just before reaching the next junction you pass a stone on your left. This is known as the 'Hangman's Stone'.

7 At the junction turn right. The surface of the track soon becomes metalled. At the next junction, the Lambourn Valley Way bends left; our route, however, continues straight ahead down a tree-lined lane. On reaching a road, at the bottom, turn left and retrace your steps back, along the Fulke Walwyn Way and the road beyond, to the Malt Shovel, which will be on the right.

Date walk completed:

....

Places of Interest

Ashdown House (National Trust), which has associations with Elizabeth of Bohemia, the sister of Charles I, is situated on the B4000 between Upper Lambourn and Ashbury. The 17th century house and garden is open on Wednesdays and Saturdays between April and October. The surrounding woodland is open all year but not on Fridays. Telephone: 01793 762209.

Lambourn, situated in the 'Valley of the Racehorse', is well known today for the training of racehorses. For centuries, however, its prosperity relied on sheep rearing. The parish church of St Michael and All Angels dates back to the 12th century. The market cross, although restored, was originally erected during the reign of Henry VI.

Hungerford

The Down Gate

Hungerford, an attractive town, has played a major role in the history of this country. It was here in 1688 that William of Orange met with politicians during his progress towards London, as a result of which James II fled to France. The town was also the venue for the meeting that led to the formation of the Kennet and Avon Canal in 1810. This walk

crosses agricultural land to the south and west of the town, providing good views. The route returns via a short section of the canal and provides an opportunity to visit the church of St Lawrence and the town centre before returning to the Down Gate.

Distance: 6½ miles

OS Explorer 158 Newbury & Hungerford GR 342683

An easy walk on fairly level ground

Starting point: The Down Gate. There is a large gravelled parking area at the edge of Hungerford Common close to the pub.

How to get there: Turn south off the A4, in Hungerford, into Bridge Street (A338). After passing under the railway, turn left into Park Street. The Down Gate is about ¼ mile along on the right, with the parking area just beyond, the other side of a cattle grid.

The **Down Gate** is a friendly 'village' inn that enjoys a prominent position on the western edge of Hungerford Common. Recently redecorated, its two internal bars display a fascinating collection of artefacts, among them tankards and blowtorches. A number of old photographs of the area adorn the walls. Owned by Arkell's Brewery, Swindon, the beers served include Arkell's 3B. Recommended amongst the good pub grub on offer is their sausage and mash, which comes in a large Yorkshire pudding. Whatever your choice a warm welcome is guaranteed.

Opening times are 11 am until 11 pm every day. Food is served from 12 noon to 2.30 pm and 6 pm to 9 pm. Morning coffee may be available from 9 am during the summer.

Telephone: 01488 682708.

The Walk

1 With your back to the road walk up the slope, between the posts at the back of the car park, and onto the common. Head for the far right-hand corner, following a faint path and ignoring a footpath on the right. At the far corner, go ahead along a short enclosed track and through a gate into a recreation park. Turn right past the cricket pavilion and follow the boundary wall of Hungerford Football Ground to reach a standing stone (war memorial). Turn right through a small Memorial Park and, with the entrance to the football ground on the right, go directly ahead across an open area and along Bulpit Lane opposite. At a crossroads turn left along Priory Avenue. At the T-junction turn right, passing Combe View on the left.

2 Where the road bends sharp right, turn left along a footpath that runs between houses to reach a field. With good views of the downs in the distance, continue ahead along the left edge of the field. Go straight over a cross track, through a gap and along the edge of the next field. At the far corner turn right. In 30 yards, at a footpath sign, turn left towards some barns. Pass between a barn and fence and then follow the track as it bends left, passing a larger barn, to reach a road.

3 Turn right along the road. Just beyond Hornhill Barn, turn right at a footpath

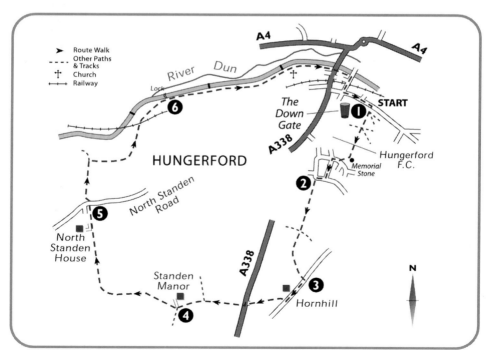

sign. When the fence on the right ends continue ahead, between fields, to reach the A338. Cross, with care, and turn left. In 25 yards turn right along a drive, signed 'Private Road to Standen Manor'. Pass a footpath, and the entrance to Standen Manor, on the right, and continue ahead, passing the William Bentley Billiards building on your left.

④ Where the main track bends left, at a track junction, continue straight ahead. Pass to the left of some large corrugated barns. Keep on the farm track as it bends right, then left, following a line of telegraph poles. On reaching a small wood, go through a gap and follow a meandering path through the trees. Follow the path between wooden fences as it bends right. Just before a five bar gate, turn right through a high swing gate and head along an enclosed path between two Christmas tree plantations. Note that the route from here to the road is a diversion to that shown on the OS map. Follow a series of enclosed paths, passing to the right of North Standen House, to reach a road.

⑤ Cross diagonally left and go along the short enclosed track opposite. At the track junction, turn right along the tree-lined track. Just before this track bends left, turn right along another track. After passing a small pond and a woodland area on the left the track leads, through a gap, to a field. Here, turn left, then right along the left edge of the field. As you approach a railway embankment look for, and cross, a stile on the left. Turn right along the base of the embankment and then up some steps to the railway. BEWARE – before crossing STOP, LOOK and LISTEN, as instructed. Go down the steps the other side and over a stile. Turn right for 10 yards then bear left along the field edge towards a red-roofed house. The River Dun is on your left.

⑥ Cross a stile on your left, near a lock, then turn right along the Kennet & Avon Canal towpath towards Hungerford. The first section of open land you pass through is Freeman's Marsh, a Site of Special Scientific Interest. The towpath takes you past Hungerford church and then Hungerford Wharf before arriving at Hungerford Bridge. If you wish to visit the town, turn right at this point otherwise remain on the towpath and follow it under the bridge. At the next canal bridge turn right up a road and over a railway crossing. Keep to the right of the Railway Tavern and follow the road up to a T-junction. Turn left, passing an attractive thatched house on the right, to return to the Down Gate and the car park.

Place of Interest
The church of St Lawrence, Hungerford, which is grade II listed, was built between 1814 and 1816 at a cost of £30,000 and replaced an earlier church on the same site. It was the first building in the area to be constructed from Bath stone, brought to Hungerford via the Kennet & Avon Canal.

Date walk completed:

....

Inkpen Common

The Crown and Garter

A tale of murder, an ancient fortress and some spectacular views set the theme of this interesting walk. Starting from Inkpen Common, the route takes you to Lower Green, past Inkpen church and across fields before climbing, quite steeply, to the top of Inkpen Hill. A gently undulating track is then followed eastwards along the ridge past Combe Gibbet and over Walbury Hill, the highest chalk cliff in Berkshire. Returning to Inkpen you pass close to West Woodhay House. Built by Inigo Jones in the 17th century, this is best seen as you descend from the ridge.

The **Crown and Garter** is a delightful 17th century country hostelry. It was once a coaching inn on one of the routes to Salisbury. Inside, the décor, although plain and simple, manages to exude plenty of character with its wooden beams, open fireplace, and wooden tables and chairs. It also has a fair sized garden. Beers include Archers Village Ale, 'Good Old Boy' from the West Berkshire Brewery and Arkell's Moonlight Ale. An interesting menu includes local produce, and all dishes are freshly prepared. There are vegetarian options. Sunday roasts are popular and it is advisable to book. The inn is closed at lunchtime on Mondays and Tuesdays.

Opening times are 12 noon to 3 pm Wednesday to Friday and 5.30 pm to 11 pm Monday to Friday; 12 noon to 11 pm on Saturday; 12 noon to 3 pm and 7 pm to 10.30 pm on Sunday. During opening times food is available from 12 noon to 2 pm (Sunday 2.30 pm) at lunchtime and 6.30 pm to 9.30 pm in the evening.

Telephone: 01488 668325.

Distance: *6¼ miles*

OS Explorer 158 Newbury & Hungerford GR 378638

An energetic walk with one steep ascent and one fairly steep descent

Starting point: The Crown and Garter. Please obtain permission to leave your car if you want to use the pub car park while you walk. Alternative parking in the village is limited.

How to get there: From the A4, halfway between Newbury and Hungerford, take the road signed to Kintbury. From there, take the road signed to Inkpen and, at a crossroads, take the Inkpen Common road. The Crown and Garter will be on your left.

The Walk

1 Leave the inn car park and turn left to the road. Cross, with care, and go along the track opposite. Pass a thatched cottage and at a path junction, fork right. In 10 yards, fork left to reach a cross-path junction. Turn left here, passing to the left of a small upright stone, to follow a path through woodland. Emerging from the trees, continue straight ahead along an unmade road. After passing a thatched cottage on the left, at a footpath sign, turn right through a swing gate and bear left across a field to the corner of a privet hedge. Turn left here to reach a road.

2 Cross the road diagonally right and continue along Pottery Lane opposite. At the far end, go past a gate and follow the track round a sharp right-hand bend. In 20 yards, turn left through a gate and down the edge of a field. Continue along the edge of a lawn and field to reach a swing gate beside a tree. Go straight across the next field to reach a road, at a bend. Continue ahead towards Manor Farm. Where the road bends left carry straight on through a gateway, passing a farm building on your left. Just 20 yards beyond the building, turn left to go through a gate and immediately turn right along an enclosed path running between a fence and a hedge. Go through two kissing gates and follow a meandering path to reach a drive and, just beyond, a road. (*To visit the Lamb pub in Lower Green, turn right along the road and, at a road junction, fork left.*)

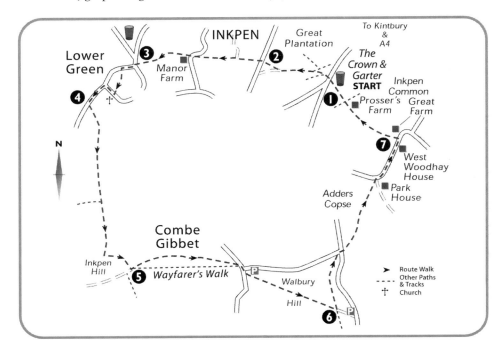

3 Turn left and swing right at the road junction. In 200 yards, turn left at a footpath sign. Pass between a house and a shed, over a stile, and along the edge of a field to reach another stile in the far corner. Cross this and head across the field towards a house, with the top of Inkpen church just visible behind it. On reaching a road at the far side, turn right. (*If you wish to visit the church, turn left and, in 20 yards, turn right.*) At the road junction, turn left for 250 yards.

4 At a footpath sign, turn left along a track. On reaching an open field, bear right along the field edge. At first there will be some trees and bushes on your right, then the path crosses open fields to reach a footpath junction. Continue straight ahead along a hedged-lined path, which soon starts to ascend gradually, to reach a gate. Go through and ascend the hillside to reach a cross path. Now, bear left and keep on this path as it goes steeply up to the summit of Inkpen Hill. There are some spectacular views of Berkshire and the Kennet Valley from the top. Go through a gate in the fence ahead and turn right to reach another gate and a broad track.

5 Turn left along the track and follow it as it skirts to the right of Combe Gibbet before descending to reach a road. There has been a hanging post at the Combe Gibbet site since 1676, when a local labourer and his mistress were executed for the murder of his wife and son. At the road junction, bear right to the track that passes to the right of a car park. In the car park there is a display board showing the history of Walbury Hill. As you ascend Walbury Hill note the earth bank you pass. This is the western rampart of the Iron Age hill fort. For the next ½ mile you will be walking within its boundary, thus getting a feel of its original size. At the summit you will be standing at the highest point in Berkshire. At the far side, continue ahead, through some trees, for 125 yards to reach a cross path and footpath sign.

6 Turn left up a bank and over a stile. Head across the field, bearing slightly left. The path passes a stile and starts to descend more steeply. There is a good view of West Woodhay House and its pond down in the valley. Go over the stile at the edge of some woodland and follow the path down through the trees to reach a road. Cross the road and continue along a meandering path opposite. On reaching a field, turn left along the edge of two fields to reach a road, at a bend. Continue straight ahead into West Woodhay, passing a footpath on the left.

7 Just before reaching Great Farm, turn left along an avenue of trees. After the houses on the right end, the track narrows and after passing Prosser's Farm, on the right, it becomes a rough track. At a path/track junction continue straight ahead to return to the inn.

Place of Interest
Walbury Hill Iron Age hill fort, covering an area of some 33 hectares, is thought to date from about 750 BC. Walbury Hill, at 974 feet, is the highest chalk cliff in England. The views from the top are quite spectacular; so choose a good clear day.

Date walk completed:

....

The Ibex

Chaddleworth, in addition to its charming cottages and period houses, has an interesting manor house and church, which although not passed on the walk are well worth seeing. Leaving the village the walk heads east along tracks and paths to Leckhampstead, where there is a rather unusual war memorial. The clock faces on the memorial

have hands made of bayonets and Roman numerals fashioned from used rifle ammunition. The route now heads north towards Brightwalton before turning west to return to Chaddleworth. Spray Wood, passed during this stretch of the walk, is a mass of bluebells during springtime.

Distance: *5 miles*

OS Explorer 158 Newbury & Hungerford GR 416773

This is a fairly level walk using paths and tracks across farmland

Starting point: The Ibex. Please obtain permission to leave your car while you walk if you use the inn car park. There is very little parking available elsewhere in the village.

How to get there: From the A338 between Hungerford and Wantage, turn off to the north of Great Shefford on the road signed to Chaddleworth.

The **Ibex** is a grade III listed building. During the 17th century it consisted of two cottages, and was part of a larger farm complex. It later became a bakery, then an off-licence before becoming an inn. Being so close to the Lambourn Downs, renowned for its racehorse training facilities and stables, there are close connections with this fraternity. The inn offers an excellent choice of menu, and the beer includes Ruddles Best and Wadworth 6X. There is a small garden at the rear of the pub.

Opening times are 11.30 am to 2.30 pm and 6.30 pm to 11 pm on Monday to Saturday; 12 noon to 3 pm and 7 pm to 10.30 pm on Sunday. Food is served from 12 noon to 2 pm every day and in the evenings on Monday to Saturday between 6.30 pm and 9.30 pm.

Telephone: 01488 638311.

The Walk

1 With your back to the Ibex, turn left down the road and bear left at the junction, signed to Boxford. After the last house on the left, turn left into Nodmore and, where this bends left, continue straight ahead along a track (Wick Lane), following it until you reach a road.

2 Turn right along the road. In 130 yards, turn left across the middle of a field, following the direction of a fingerpost. At the far side, go through a gap in the hedge then bear left across another field. Keep to the right at a hedge corner and continue ahead, with a hedge on your left and young saplings on your

right. There are some good views on the right. Where the hedge on your left turns left, at a footpath junction, bear diagonally right across the field. Go through a gap and maintain direction across a second field. Go through another gap on the far side and then turn left along a bridleway. Pass Manor Farm and continue along Manor Lane to reach a road junction, with a small church just opposite.

3 Turn left up Shop Lane into Leckhampstead. Pass the Stag pub and at the village green bear left. Do not forget to look closely at the war memorial on the green. Follow the road round to the left and, in 50 yards just past a 30mph sign, turn right across the grass to join a track.

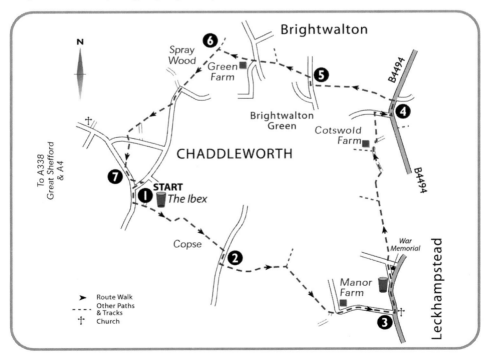

Continue along the track, ignoring a footpath going off left. At a farm-vehicle junction, bear right, then right again to reach a track T-junction. Here, turn left towards Cotswold Farm. Just before the farm, ignore another path going off left and continue ahead to pass to the right of the farm. Where the farm track bends right take a path going left, at a footpath sign. Go through a gate and along the left edge of a field. Go through another gate and across the middle of the next field to reach a road. Turn right to the B4494 junction.

❹ Turn left along the B4494. In 300 yards, just before a small enclosure, turn left up the edge of the field, then between fields. Keep to the right of a hedge and continue ahead towards the houses of Brightwalton Green. Pass to the right of a tennis court and, at the field corner, continue ahead past a wooden shed to emerge at a road. Turn right here.

❺ In 100 yards, just past a house called Sheardon, turn left at a footpath sign. Pass Field Cottage and immediately turn left along a short enclosed path. Cross a stile and continue along the field edge, ignoring a path going off left. Go over another stile and ahead across the middle of the next field, aiming just to the right of some green-roofed sheds. Brightwalton church is visible to your right. At the far side, go through a gate, over a road and across the green opposite. Continue ahead over a second road and head towards some barns at Green Farm. Just before the barns, turn right towards a thatched cottage; then turn left to pass to the right of a large barn. Maintain direction across the middle of a field towards Spray Wood.

❻ On reaching the edge of the wood, turn left. Spray Wood, now on your right, is quite a spectacular sight during spring due to its abundance of bluebells. On reaching a road, at a bend, continue straight ahead. In 150 yards, at a footpath sign, bear right up a path between fields. At the far side, go ahead along a narrow path running between a hedge and a wooden fence. Go over a stile and turn left along the field edge. Chaddleworth House can be seen on your right. Go through a gate in the far corner, over a road, and continue along a path opposite, passing to the left of the village hall. Immediately after passing a playground, bear right across a field. At the far side, the path drops down to a road. (*To visit the church, turn right uphill.*)

❼ Turn left down Tower Hill. Just after passing two thatched cottages on the left, at Boxhedge Cottage, bear left along a narrow path running between privet hedges to emerge at a road, with the Ibex directly opposite.

Places of Interest

Chaddleworth church has a memorial dedicated to the Nelson family. In the church register there is a reference to a member who fought in the English Civil War.

The redundant **church of St Thomas, Great Shefford**, south-west of Chaddleworth, situated in a water meadow, dates back to the Norman period and contains the 15th/16th century tombs of the Fettiplace family.

Date walk completed:

....

Crockham Heath

The Craven Arms

mansion, built in 1660, was destroyed by fire. The longer route crosses over the new A34 Newbury Bypass and heads towards the town before turning up to Wash Common where, in September 1643, the first of Newbury's two Civil War battles took place. Field paths and lanes are followed back to the finish.

Starting from the tiny hamlet of Crockham Heath, situated between Enborne and Hamstead Marshall, this is a walk with great historical interest. The route takes in a small section of Hamstead Park, which was designed by the eminent Dutch architect Sir Balthazar Gerbierk for Sir William Craven in the 17th century. A magnificent

The **Craven Arms** was built on the Craven Estate. Its low wooden beams indicate that the building is late 17th or early 18th century. The bar and dining areas are carpeted and the latter are sub-divided into small separate sections. Interesting paintings and prints adorn the walls. It has a large beer garden, with a children's play area, and a large car park. Beers include Wadworth 6X, Henry's IPA and a seasonal ale. A good varied selection of food is available and is served in generous quantities by pleasant and friendly staff.

Distance: 3¾ or 6½ miles

OS Explorer 158 Newbury & Hungerford GR 427648

This is a relatively easy walk with one gradual ascent and descent

Starting point: The Craven Arms. The pub has a large car park.

How to get there: From the A343 in Newbury, take a minor road, Enborne Road, west to Enborne. After passing Enborne church, you will reach the Craven Arms on the corner at the next road junction.

Opening times are 12 noon to 3 pm and 5 pm to 11 pm on Tuesday to Thursday; 12 noon to 11 pm on Friday and Saturday; 12 noon to 10.30 pm on Sunday. Food is served from 12 noon to 2 pm and 6.30 pm to 8.45 pm on Tuesday to Thursday and from 12 noon to 8.45 pm on Friday, Saturday and Sunday.

Telephone: 01635 253336.

The Walk

❶ Leave the pub car park and turn right. At the road junction turn right again. Follow the lane for just over ¼ mile to reach a footpath sign on the left, beside the entrance drive to Crockhamheath Farm. Go through a swing gate and bear right across the field to a fence corner. Turn left here to pass to the right of the farm buildings. Go through a swing gate and continue ahead across two fields. The path goes through some trees and bushes to a squeeze stile at the far side. Cross and then turn left along the field edge. Go through a gap in the corner, over a small stream, and then bear half-left across a wild meadow to cross a stile and footbridge. A short enclosed section leads to a stile. Cross this and turn left up the edge of two fields to reach a road. Turn left for 20 yards then turn right along a track, through trees, to reach the boundary fence of Hamstead Park. Go through a swing gate and ahead along an old grassy drive for 150 yards to reach a path junction.

❷ Turn right across the grass to a metalled drive. Note the large white stone you pass. A plaque on it reveals that it is dedicated to American troopers who set up camp in the park in 1944, prior to the D-Day landings. Follow the drive through Hamstead Park until you emerge at a road. The 12th century Enborne church, directly opposite, is well worth a visit. Turn left and at the next road junction, turn right along Church Lane. Look out for Old Lane Cottage on the left.

❸ Turn left, here, along an enclosed path. Go through a squeeze stile and ahead down the edge of a field. Cross a stile and footbridge in the far corner and

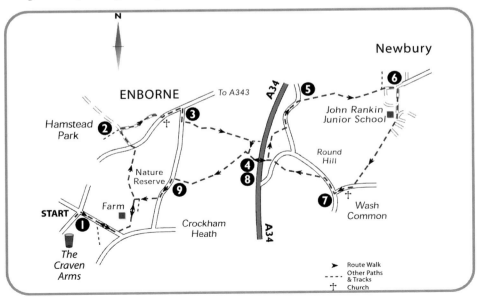

go straight across the next field. After crossing a stile and earth bridge go through a narrow band of trees to reach another stile. Cross this and turn right to reach a stile at the foot of the footbridge over the A34.

4 *For the shorter walk turn right here and follow the directions from point 8.* For the longer walk; cross the bridge over the A34. At the far side, turn left at a footpath sign. The path runs parallel with the A34 before bending right to a stile and footbridge. Cross these and bear quarter-left across a field, keeping to the left of some houses to reach a road. Turn left along the road until you reach a sharp left-hand bend.

5 Leave the road at this point and go straight ahead along a hedge-lined path. The hedges eventually give way to open fields. At a small copse continue straight ahead. The path eventually merges with a rough road, with houses on the right and a playing field on the left. Carry on until you reach a road junction.

6 Turn right along Oaken Grove. At the end bear left, then right, following a path that takes you past John Rankin Junior School, where it joins with a road. Where the road bends left, bear right at a footpath sign. Go through a swing gate and follow the path up the edge of a large field. The fields to your right, including Round Hill, are where the Civil War battles took place. At the top end, go along an enclosed path to reach a road. Turn right through Wash Common to reach a lane on the right.

7 Turn right here. In 250 yards, turn left over a stile and bear diagonally right

across the field. There is an excellent panoramic view from here. Cross a stile in the bottom corner and turn right along the field edge to reach a lane. Cross this and the stile opposite and follow a track that leads back to the bridge over the A34. Cross this and the stile on the far side, then turn left.

8 Go straight across two fields, then along an enclosed section, bending left then right, before going along the right-hand edge of another field. Just before the far corner, turn right then left to cross a stile and footbridge. Now follow an enclosed fenced path to reach a road.

9 Turn left along the road, passing Avery's Pightle Nature Reserve on the right. After passing the entrance to Villa Fiorita, turn right over a stile, just to the left of a track. Follow the path along the edge of two fields. Just before the far corner turn left. The walk now retraces the route back past Crockhamheath Farm and out to the road, where you turn right following it back to the Craven Arms, which will be on the left.

Place of Interest

Highclere Castle, situated just to the south of Newbury, is the ancestral home of the earls of Carnarvon. It was the 5th Earl who, with Howard Carter, uncovered the tomb of Tutankhamun. The castle, created by Sir Charles Barry, who designed the Houses of Parliament, is considered to be one of the finest Victorian houses in the country. It is open on specific days between July and September. Telephone: 01635 253210.

Date walk completed:

....

Bagnor 6

The Blackbird

of Donnington Castle, look at the flora and fauna to be found on Snelsgrove Common, and visit Winterbourne village. The return to Bagnor, across agricultural land, presents some magnificent views across the Kennet and Lambourn valleys. To complete your day out why not take the opportunity to visit the nearby Watermill Theatre?

For a perfect day out in Berkshire, Bagnor has to feature very high on the list. Start the day with this interesting historical and environmental walk, on which you can visit the ruins

Distance: *6 miles*

OS Explorer 158 Newbury & Hungerford GR 454693

This is a moderate walk through undulating countryside

Starting point: The Blackbird inn. Please obtain permission to leave your car while you walk. Alternative parking is available at Donnington Castle (point 2) or Snelsgrove Country Park (point 3).

How to get there: Bagnor is situated 2 miles north-west of Newbury. From the A4 in Newbury follow the brown 'Watermill Theatre' signs to Bagnor. The Blackbird will be on the right before you reach the Watermill.

The **Blackbird,** situated in the pretty village of Bagnor with the River Lambourn directly opposite, is one of those friendly village pubs that is always a delight to visit. The present building replaced a thatched inn that succumbed to fire during the early 20th century. The choice of food varies from sandwiches and ploughman's through to various fish dishes and Sunday roasts. Vegetarians are also catered for. Beer includes Butts ales, West Berkshire ales and Fuller's London Pride. Booking is essential especially at weekends.

Opening times are 12 noon to 11 pm on Monday to Saturday and 12 noon to 10.30 pm on Sunday. Food is served from 12 noon to 2 pm and 6 pm to 9 pm on Monday to Saturday and 12 noon to 4 pm on Sunday.

Telephone: 01635 40638.

The Walk

1 With your back to the inn turn left and follow the track that runs between houses. At the end bear left through a gate and up a concrete track over the A34. At the far side ignore a track on the right and swing left uphill to a cross track. Go straight over and in 6 yards turn right through woodland. At the far side, go through a gate and swing left, ascending steeply to Donnington Castle.

2 Pass to the right of the castle and go through a gate. Turn left. Pass Castle Farm and immediately after the last barn turn left back over the A34. At the far side swing right, ascending gradually until the drive becomes a grassy track. Ignore a left fork to the golf course and continue ahead between fences. At the far end of the golf course, carry straight on. Pass to the left of a house and, just beyond, go through a gate into Snelsgrove Common and continue ahead. Go over a cross track to a junction. Follow the path straight ahead, passing a fire control tower on your left and then across an open boggy section. At the far side go ahead into the trees and at a path junction, bear right. When you are in sight of a road look for, and go through, a gate on your left. You should now be at the entrance to Snelsgrove Common car park.

3 With your back to the road, go through the vehicle barrier and fork right along a tarmac track, passing car park areas on your left. Go through a kissing gate and in 30 yards veer right along a gravel track. At a track junction, fork right and in 10 yards fork left. Go over a cross track and descend, passing beneath power lines, into woodland. Go over a second cross track and continue descending to reach a stile. Do not cross but turn right, keeping the fence on your left. Ignore a stile on the left and, after crossing a small gully, maintain direction to ascend fairly steeply, through trees, to a gate and lane.

4 Turn left. At a corner of the wood on the right, opposite a house on the left, turn right along the edge of the wood to go through a swing gate. Continue along the edge of the next field and through another swing gate. Turn left along the field edge and in 20 yards bear right across three fields, aiming towards the houses of Winterbourne. At the far side of the third field, with the houses fairly close on your left, turn left, crossing a bridge over a small stream, to reach a road. Turn right.

5 In 120 yards turn left to join a track running between fields. As you approach Lower Farm, continue straight ahead passing to the right of the farm. On reaching a wood the path passes through the corner of the wood then turns left along the wood edge. In 100 yards, where the field edge bends right, bear left up to a gate. Go through and turn right. Follow the field edge round in a big arc, ignoring a gate on the right. With a wood, and then a strip of woodland, on the right, maintain direction along the edge of three fields to reach a road.

6 Turn right along the road. In 250 yards, turn left over a stile into woodland. Go along a track for 30 yards then fork left onto a narrow path through the trees. Where a wider track joins from the right, continue straight ahead. At a small waymarked post, fork right to a stile in

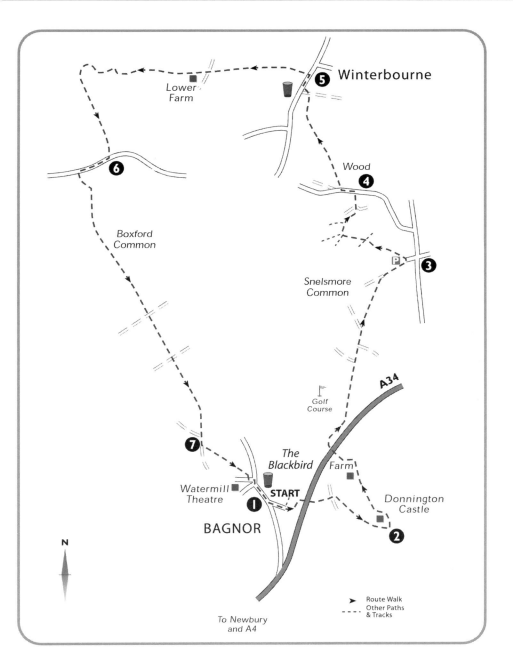

Winterbourne

Lower
Farm

5

6

Wood

4

Boxford
Common

3

Snelsmore
Common

A34

Golf
Course

7

*The
Blackbird*   Farm

Watermill
Theatre   **START**

Donnington
Castle

1

2

BAGNOR

N

➤ Route Walk
- - - - Other Paths
& Tracks

To Newbury
and A4

Donnington Castle

eventually descending to emerge at the edge of a field. Keep to the right-hand side of a hedgerow directly in front of you. Continue ahead over two cross tracks, through a young plantation, and across fields. In approximately ½ mile the track descends between hedges. At the bottom, where a track joins from the right, carry straight on for 50 yards.

7 Turn left through a gap in the hedge and bear diagonally right across the field to a gap in the far right corner. Go through an enclosed area between gardens, over a stile; then turn right to reach a road. Turn left and almost immediately bend right at a road junction. At the next junction bend left over a stream and follow the road back to the Blackbird.

the right-hand fence. Go diagonally left across the field to another stile, then across the middle of a large field to go over a stile in the far right-hand corner. Follow the path through woodland,

Date walk completed:

....

Place of Interest
Donnington Castle. The magnificent gatehouse is all that remains of a castle that has been on this site since the 14th century. The castle ruin is open, free, to the public at any time.

The Harrow Inn

W est Ilsley, a delightful village nestling in a fold of the Berkshire Downs, has been involved in training racehorse winners, including those owned by the Queen, for many years. Starting from the village the route takes you past the Old Rectory, where Charles I was reputed to have stayed in 1644. After passing the 17th century church the walk heads south towards Windmill Down, passing West Ilsley Stables. A change of direction takes you northwards to the Ridgeway, which is followed in a westerly direction. A good clear day is required to fully appreciate the excellent views that are available.

The **Harrow Inn** has historic connections with Morland's, the brewers – it was here, in 1711, that the brewery was founded. The inn has an open plan bar, recently painted in green and terracotta. The walls are adorned with a small collection of horse paintings, featuring many that were champions in their day. Food is mainly simple fare and varies from sandwiches, French rolls and sausage and mash at lunchtime, with more substantial dishes being available in the evening. Roast dinners are available on Sundays, at lunchtime. Beers include Greene King IPA and Abbot Ale and Ruddles Smooth.

Opening times are 12 noon to 3 pm and 6 pm to 11 pm each day in the summer – closed Sunday and Monday evenings in winter. Food is served between 12 and 2 pm on Monday to Sunday and between 7 pm and 9 pm on Tuesday to Sunday.

Telephone: 01635 281260.

Distance: *7 miles*

OS Explorer 170 Abingdon, Wantage & Vale of White Horse
GR 470826

An easy walk on level ground

Starting point: The Harrow Inn. A certain amount of roadside parking is available near the inn and in the village.

How to get there: Turn off the A34 Newbury to Oxford road, 5 miles north of the M4 at junction 13, following the signs to West Ilsley. The Harrow Inn is situated at the western end of the village, and will be on the right.

27

The Walk

❶ With your back to the pub turn left along Main Street. Pass the Old Rectory and All Saints' church, both on the right. Shortly after going round a sharp right-hand bend, turn right into Church Way. On reaching a road junction, with the entrance to Keeper's Stables on your right, turn right along a service road leading to Hodcott House and West Ilsley Stables.

❷ Just before reaching the house, turn right up a track. After crossing a cattle grid, turn left and follow the track that takes you around the stables, to a track

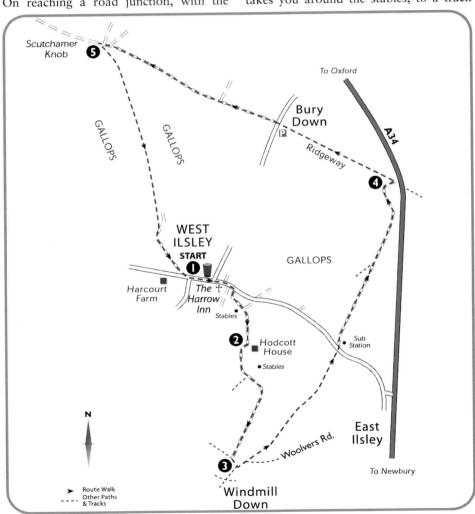

junction. Here, fork left and, almost immediately, turn right along a hedge-lined track. Views of the downs soon open up ahead of you. Directly ahead is Windmill Down. One can only assume that it once had a windmill, long since succumbed to the ravages of time. After walking for about ½ mile you reach a T-junction. Turn left to reach another T-junction and a byway sign. The cross track is called Woolvers Road.

3 Turn left along the track. In 60 yards leave Woolvers Road by bearing left onto a narrow footpath. Follow this tree-lined path, running between fields, until you reach a road. Turn left for 30 yards then cross the road, with care, to a footpath sign and track on the other side. Pass a small electricity sub-station on your right and follow a wide track that ascends gradually up Hodcott Down. Over to your right you can see and hear the traffic whizzing along the A34. At the top, the track bends left, then right towards the A34. As you near the right-hand fence you reach a cross track. This is the Ridgeway.

4 Turn left along the Ridgeway, away from the A34. The walk now remains on this ancient thoroughfare for the next 1¾ miles. There are excellent views to your right, with Didcot Power Station, Harwell, its Research Centre, and other Oxfordshire villages clearly visible. At the top of Bury Down, go through a car parking area, across a minor road, and continue ahead along the Ridgeway, now almost as wide as a modern day motorway. Pass a track on the right and head for a distant hilltop copse, called Scutchamer Knob. Just before the Ridgeway starts to make the long gradual ascent up to the copse, and just after passing a track on the right, turn left at a cross track.

5 Pass between two white posts, and cross a grassy gallop to a fence on the far side. Keeping the fence on your right, turn left and follow the fence round as it bends right. Ignore a gallop, going off to the right and continue ahead along a grassy track, with a wire fence on your right. Once again you have some excellent panoramic views of the surrounding countryside, especially towards the downs to the south. The track gradually narrows and starts to ascend, fairly steeply, towards Harcourt Farm. Before reaching the farm, however, the track bends left and soon emerges at a road. Turn left here and in 50 yards you reach the Harrow Inn and the finish of the walk.

Date walk completed:

....

Places of Interest

East Ilsley, situated to the east of the A34, was once an important sheep market town. The sheep fairs that were held there during the 17th century received a charter from James I. At one period the only sheep market that was larger and more important than that of East Ilsley, was Smithfield's in London. A commemoration stone stands on the site where the sheep were penned.

Farnborough, situated to the west of West Ilsley, has a 15th century church with one of its windows dedicated to the memory of John Betjeman, who once lived in the village.

The Fox Inn

story *The Fox*? The walk visits the village of Oare, passing the church described by another literary 'giant' – John Betjeman – as 'a Victorian gem set in the Berkshire countryside'. During the latter part of the walk you pass Grimsbury Castle, a hill fort that predates Roman times. With some working wood-land to negotiate the walk is both interesting and gently challenging.

For two years of his life, the author D.H. Lawrence lived in the village – at Chapel Farm Cottage. It is said that he quite often imbibed at the Fox Inn. Is it mere coincidence that during the period he lived in Hermitage, he wrote his

Distance: *5½ miles*

OS Explorer 158 Newbury & Hungerford GR 509731

This is a gently undulating walk across farmland and through woods

Starting point: The Fox Inn car park. Please obtain permission to leave your car while you walk.

How to get there: Leave the M4 at junction 13 and take the A34 towards Oxford. Leave this at the first junction and turn right. The road goes back over the M4. On reaching the A4009, turn left into Hermitage. The Fox will be the second inn on the right.

The **Fox Inn** building dates back to the 16th or early 17th century. Internally the bars have wooden beams and the main bar area has a good collection of horse brasses. One of the smaller bars has a pool table and there is a separate dining area. Beers include Courage Director's, Bass and two guest ales. Lunchtime snacks include baguettes, jacket potatoes and omelettes. A more substantial menu is also available, especially during the evening. There is a small garden to enjoy on warm days. Overnight accommodation is also available.

Opening times are 12 noon to 2.30 pm and 5 pm to 11 pm on Monday to Friday; 12 noon to 11 pm on Saturday; 12 noon to 10.30 pm on Sunday. Food is served between 12 noon and 2 pm daily, and between 6.15 pm and 9.30 pm on Tuesday to Saturday.

Telephone: 01635 201545.

The Walk

1 Leave the pub car park and turn right along the B4009. In 100 yards, turn left up a path into Roebuck Wood. Keep to the main path through the wood. Where a path joins from the left, continue straight ahead. Ignore a path veering off to the right and maintain direction, soon passing a bench seat. At a footpath sign, continue ahead to join a drive, just after passing a house on the left. In 50 yards, at a footpath sign, turn right and descend to a lane. Turn right into Oare. Pass Oare church to reach the fence corner of Oare Cottage, on the right.

2 Turn right here, passing a small pond on your left. Go over a stile and head along the left edge of a field towards Little Hungerford. After crossing another stile, turn right and follow the field edge, bending left, with a school on the right, to reach a road. Turn right and in 150 yards, turn left along Chapel Lane. Shortly after passing Deacon's Lane, on the right, the lane bends sharp right.

3 (*If you wish to see Chapel Farm Cottage, remain on the road until you reach Pond Lane on the right. The cottage is on the furthest corner.*) To continue the walk, do not follow the road round but carry straight ahead on a path leading through some trees. Go over a stile and continue along the field edge, with a notice on the fence on your left indicating 'Deep Water'. Cross another stile and walk along a path running just inside the edge of a wood. At the far end, with the M4 directly ahead of you, go over a stile then bear right across the corner of a field to another stile at the corner of a strip of woodland.

4 Walk along the field edge, with the wood directly on your right, until you reach a road. Turn left and, in 80 yards, turn right past a barrier and along a track. At a path/track junction continue ahead. A sign on the left states 'Box Wood, Eling Estate'. Remain on the main track until you join the drive of Wellhouse Farm, following it out to its junction with a road. Cross the road and continue along the byway opposite, ignoring a path going off right, until you reach another minor road.

5 Turn right. Just past a telephone kiosk, turn left onto a metalled track, signed to Boar's Hole Farm. Follow the track as it bends left, then right to pass between the farmhouse and some barns, to reach West Wood. Continue along the edge of the wood, which will be on your left, and just before the track bends left at the far corner of the wood, turn right through an open gateway onto a path running along the right-hand edge of a field. Aim just to the right of a house, visible on the far side. Just beyond the house you reach a track junction.

6 Turn right through a metal gate. At the first junction, fork right and continue ahead, soon passing over a small stream. Ignore a turning on the left and stay on the main track until you reach the next junction. Here, turn left along an avenue of Christmas trees, with a small stream running on your right. Go straight over the first cross track, gradually ascending to reach a second cross track, with a small pond just to your right. Turn right here. Ignore a faint path veering off left and continue along the main track for another 100 yards before turning left up another track. At the next cross track turn right,

31

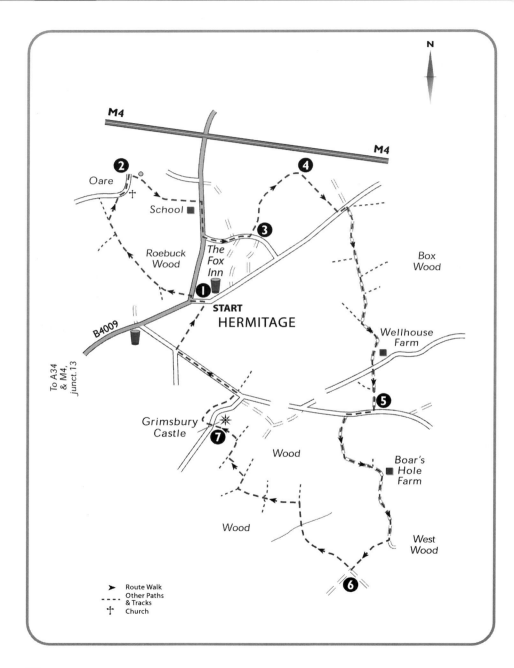

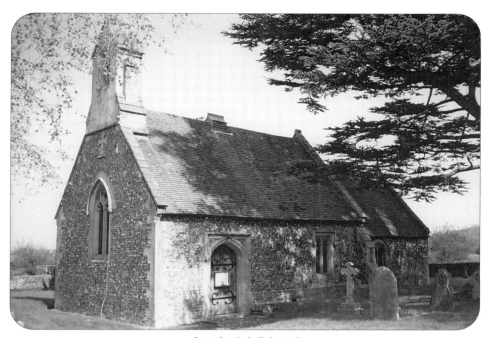

Oare church, 'a little gem'

descending then ascending up to another cross track. Turn left and follow the track, passing a house on the right, to a road.

7 Turn right to a T-junction and turn left. After passing the Hermitage road sign, and just before the old railway bridge, turn right along a path running alongside the foot of the embankment. At the next road, turn left and in 100 yards turn right to the Fox Inn.

Place of Interest

The Living Rainforest, Hampstead Norreys is situated on the B4009 a few miles north of Hermitage. Here, one can experience the wonders of a real rainforest; with its many exotic plants and fascinating and endangered animals and insects, all under cover. Open daily (except Christmas Day and Boxing Day) between 10 am and 5.15 pm. Telephone: 01635 202444.

Date walk completed:

Aldworth
The Bell Inn

No visit to Aldworth is complete without a visit to St Mary's church to see the nine recumbent stone effigies of the de le Beche family, known as the 'Aldworth Giants'. The family lived in the village during the 13th and 14th centuries. Buried in the churchyard are Lawrence Binyon, author

of the Remembrance Day words 'They shall grow not old', and Leonard Rossiter. From the church the route heads over the downs, from where there is a good view down towards the Goring Gap. Following a long descent along the Ridgeway the route climbs up to Westridge – and to Southridge on the longer walk – before returning to Aldworth.

The **Bell Inn**, one of Berkshire's classic pubs, has evolved from a 14th century five-bay cruck manor hall. Members of the same family have run it for over 200 years. Enter and you step back in time. A glass-panelled hatch takes the place of the more conventional bar. The taproom on the left, with its original wooden benches, tables and a 300 year old one-handed clock, is a joy. The menu takes the form of warm crusty rolls filled with locally produced meats, or crab specially brought up from Devon. Beers on offer include Old Tyler, Wren's and Maggs Magnificent Mild. In good weather these can be enjoyed in a pleasant garden at the side of the pub.

Distance: *4¾ or 6½ miles*

OS Explorer 158 Newbury & Hungerford and 170 Abingdon, Wantage & Vale of White Horse GR 555796

A moderate walk with one long descent and one fairly steep ascent

Starting point: The Bell Inn. The car park at the rear of the pub has limited parking. Spaces are available elsewhere in the village for careful parking.

How to get there: Aldworth is 2½ miles south-west of Streatley on the B4009. Turn northwards off the main road to get to the pub.

Opening times are 11 am to 3 pm and 6 pm to 11 pm on Tuesday to Saturday; 12 noon to 3 pm and 7 pm to 10.30 pm on Sunday. Food is served is served from 11 am to 2.45 pm and 6 pm to 10.45 pm on Tuesday to Saturday; 12 noon to 2.45 pm and 7 pm to 10.15 pm on Sunday. Note that the Bell is not open on Mondays.

Telephone: *01635 578272.*

The Walk

❶ With the pub behind you cross to the road opposite. The well on the left is thought to be 372 feet deep. Follow the road down to reach St Mary's church on the right. Go through the lychgate into the churchyard. To visit the graves of Laurence Binyon and Leonard Rossiter turn right off the path then right again towards the hedge. Return to the path and follow it round to pass the church entrance on the right. Go through a gate in the corner of the churchyard and then turn right along a wide track. Ignore a

footpath on the left and remain on the main track as it bends right between fields to reach a lane. Turn left for 300 yards.

❷ At a signpost, 'Warren Farm', turn right down a track and follow it as it bends sharp left. Pause here to admire the excellent view looking down the valley towards Streatley and the Goring Gap. Remain on the main track for ½ mile to reach a T- junction (the Ridgeway).

❸ Turn right and, ignoring a path going off left, follow the Ridgeway downhill. At the bottom the Ridgeway levels out and

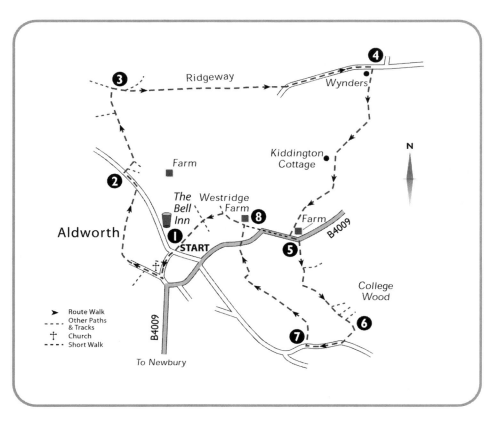

35

its surface becomes metalled. Continue ahead for another ½ mile and look for a house on the right called 'Wynders'.

4 Immediately after passing the entrance, turn right at a footpath sign. The path, enclosed at first, bends left then right before emerging onto open fields. Continue ahead on a clear path towards Kiddington Cottage, hidden behind a small clump of trees. Pass to the right of the trees to reach a track. Turn left, passing to the left of the cottage, and continue ahead. The track, rising gently at first, soon ascends more steeply through woodland. At the top continue ahead to pass between some farm buildings and stables to reach the A4009. *For the shorter walk turn right along the road. Where the road bends left continue straight ahead along a wide track past Westridge Farm. Here you rejoin the longer walk, at point 8.*

5 To continue with the longer walk, cross the road, with care, and turn left. In 100 yards, where the road bends sharp left, turn right down a tree-lined track. At the bottom, where the track turns left to a cottage, continue straight ahead on a narrow path into woodland. Ignore a path going right into a field and continue ahead as indicated by the yellow marker on a post. The path runs just inside the right-hand edge of a narrow strip of wood. Where a gap in the trees opens up either side of the path, maintain direction up into College Wood. Ignore all paths going left and continue ahead to reach and go through a wooden barrier.

6 Now, turn right and, ignoring a path going off left, continue ahead to reach a lane at a bend. Carry straight on along the lane for 400 yards to reach a track (signposted) on the right.

7 Turn right along the hedge-lined track. In 200 yards, where you go through a gap, look for the remains of an old earthwork, known as Grim's Ditch, on the right. The track now becomes more tree-lined, as it runs just inside the edge of Portobello Wood. When the wood ends continue straight ahead. The track bends right, then left, around a disused pit, before reaching the A4009 at Westridge Green. Turn right for 30 yards then cross the road to a track opposite. Follow this to reach a cross track at Westridge Farm. Turn left here.

8 Continue along the track for 250 yards. At a footpath sign turn left across the middle of a field. At the far side go over a cross track, through a gap in the hedge, and then bear left across the next field. At a hedge corner, continue ahead keeping the hedge on your left. Go through a gate in the field corner and along an enclosed path to reach a road. Turn right to return to the Bell Inn.

Place of Interest
Basildon Park (National Trust) is an attractive 18th century Palladian mansion built by John Carr situated on the west side of the A329 between Pangbourne and Streatley. It is set in extensive parkland, which has a number of waymarked trails. It is open from April until the end of October but not on Mondays or Tuesdays. Telephone: 0118 984 3040.

Date walk completed:
....

country. This fascinating walk starts at Aldermaston Wharf where you can visit the Kennet and Avon Canal Visitor Centre when it is open. A short stretch along the canal and the River Kennet leads you past Padworth Mill. It then takes to slightly higher ground before dropping down into Aldermaston village. The walk returns via fields, road and canal towpath, back to Aldermaston Wharf.

Although Aldermaston is recognised for the 'Ban the Bomb' marches that took place in the 1960s, the village has another claim to fame. It was here, in 1840, that John Staid, a local schoolmaster, propagated the first William pear to be grown in this

The **Butt Inn** is thought to have obtained its name from the archery butts that were once positioned in the field opposite. Being close to the Kennet and Avon Canal this delightful inn attracts a good number of walkers and boating enthusiasts, especially during the summer months. Pub fare ranges from sandwiches, baguettes or a ploughman's to the more exotic Fisherman's Medley. Traditional roasts are available on a Sunday. Beers include Flowers, Boddingtons and Butts Bitter.

Distance: *6 miles*

OS Explorer 159 Reading, Wokingham & Pangbourne
GR 600669

This is mainly a flat route with one short gradual ascent

Starting point: The Butt Inn car park. Please obtain permission to leave your car while you are walking.

How to get there: From the A4 between Reading and Newbury, approx 4 miles west of junction 12 of the M4, turn southwards onto the A340. The Butt Inn is on the right a short distance after crossing the Kennet and Avon Canal at Aldermaston Wharf.

Opening times are 12 noon to 2.30 pm and 6 pm to 11 pm on Monday to Saturday; 12 noon to 5 pm and 7 pm to 10.30 pm on Sunday. Open all day during the summer. Food is served at lunchtime between 12 noon and 2 pm on Monday to Saturday and 12 noon to 3 pm on Sunday. In the evening it is available from 6 pm to 9 pm on Tuesday to Thursday; 6.30 pm to 9.30 pm on Friday and Saturday; 7 pm to 9 pm on Sunday.

Telephone: 0118 971 2129.

The Walk

1 Leave the pub car park and turn left along the A340. Cross the bridge over the Kennet and Avon Canal and immediately turn right onto the towpath. Pass the Canal Visitor Centre on the left and continue along the towpath past Aldermaston Wharf to Froudes Swing Bridge.

2 Leave the towpath here and turn right over the canal. Walk along Padworth Lane, passing the entrance to Aldermaston Quarry on the right, to reach Padworth Bridge and the River Kennet.

3 Just before the bridge, bear right down the bank, through a squeeze stile and continue ahead with the River Kennet on your left. Padworth House can be seen on the hillside on the opposite side of the river. As you approach Padworth Mill the path narrows and meanders through some scrub and trees to reach a track (Mill Lane). The old mill is just to your left. Turn right along Mill Lane for 30 yards to reach a footpath sign.

4 Turn sharp left here along a narrow fenced footpath, bending left and right before crossing the River Kennet via four footbridges. After crossing the last bridge continue ahead around some bushes to a

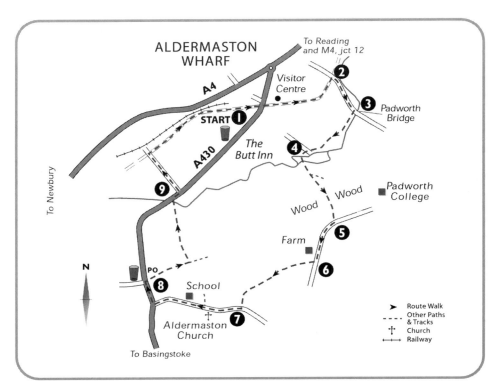

stile at the edge of a field. Cross the field to reach a footpath junction at the far side. Continue straight ahead across this next field and at the far side go over a stile and earth bridge to follow a narrow path that soon widens and ascends gradually through woodland to reach a road.

5 Turn right uphill. Pass Upper Church Farm on the right and continue ahead for another 70 yards to reach a house on the left called 'Ladywood'.

6 Here, turn right over a stile and descend down the right side of a meadow. Go through a gate, just to the right of a larger gate, and continue down an enclosed strip of land between two fields. At the bottom, go over a stile on the left and immediately turn right along a path that skirts around a small, secluded pond before bending right to a stile at the edge of a field. Cross the field, keeping just to the left of a couple of mid-field trees. Maintain direction across the next field to go over another stile before bearing left along a wire fence to reach a road.

7 Turn right along the road. Pass Aldermaston church and the entrance to Aldermaston Park on the left and as you descend towards the village centre look out for Cedars School on the right. A plaque about the William pear is on the schoolhouse wall. On reaching a road junction, note the old Lodge Gates of Aldermaston Court on the left. Now bear right, keeping to the right-hand pavement, and head towards the attractive 17th century bell-towered Hind's Head Inn, which you will see directly ahead of you. This old coaching inn once had its own gaol.

8 When you are directly opposite the inn, turn right into Fisherman's Lane, passing to the right of the village post office and a telephone box. In 500 yards turn left over a stile. The path crosses three fields, each divided by a stile, stream and a footbridge. At the far side of the third field go through a squeeze stile, cross another small stream and then bear left through a small copse to reach a gate and road. Turn right, over the River Kennet, and in 150 yards cross the road (with care) to Frouds Lane opposite.

9 Follow Frouds Lane, passing Frouds Farm and a Flower Barn on the left, to reach the Kennet and Avon Canal at Frouds Bridge. Turn right onto the towpath and follow the canal back to Aldermaston Lock and, just beyond, the A340. Turn right to return to the Butt Inn.

Places of Interest
The Kennet and Avon Canal Visitor Centre, which is open between 1 April and 31 October, offers refreshments, souvenirs and information about the canal and other British waterways. Admission is free. Telephone: 0118 971 2868.

The Vyne (National Trust), situated at Sherborne St John, between Aldermaston and Basingstoke, is a 16th century house built for Lord Sandys, Henry VIII's Lord Chamberlain. It contains a fascinating Tudor chapel and a Palladian staircase. Telephone: 01256 881337.

Date walk completed:

The Cross Keys

found the Berkshire countryside so idyllic in this area that it had inspired him to write his delightful story, *The Wind in the Willows*. He moved to Pangbourne in 1924, setting up home at Church Cottage, near to the start of the walk. He died in 1932 and although his funeral was held at the church of St James the Less, Pangbourne, he is actually buried in a cemetery in Oxford.

Pangbourne was, and still is, a fashionable riverside settlement. The author Kenneth Grahame had

Passing through the delightful riverside meadows and woodlands you may see some of the animals he based his characters on.

Distance: *6 miles*

OS Explorer 159 Reading, Wokingham & Pangbourne
GR 634765

A moderate walk with one short steep ascent and one long gradual ascent

Starting point: The public car park (Pay & Display), near the village hall, in the centre of Pangbourne. The Cross Keys has a small car park, which is usually full.

How to get there: Pangbourne lies at the junction of the A329 Reading–Wantage road and the A340. Approaching from junction 12 of the M4, follow the A4 west and at the second roundabout turn north along the A340. As you enter Pangbourne, the Cross Keys is on the right. The public car park is on the left, just beyond the A329 Reading turning.

The **Cross Keys,** which dates back to the 16th century, is a delightful inn situated in the centre of Pangbourne directly opposite the church of St James the Less. The interior of the pub consists of a number of small rooms, all with low wood-beamed ceilings. There is a patio and gazebo at the rear where you can relax and watch the River Pang flow by. Traditional Sunday roasts are very popular and you are advised to book for these. Sandwiches, baguettes, snacks, light meals or something more substantial are also available.

Opening times are 10 am until 11 pm daily (Sunday 10.30 pm). Food is served from 12 noon to 3 pm and 6 pm to 10.30 pm on Monday to Friday and all day on Saturday and Sunday.

Telephone: 0118 984 3268.

The Walk

1 Leave the car park via the pedestrian exit in the right-hand corner and turn right towards the mini roundabout. Here, cross the road to go along the High Street opposite. At the road junction, with the George Hotel on the corner, turn left into Whitchurch Road. Pass under the railway and follow the road as it bends right. Just past the entrance to a car park on the right, turn right down some steps (signed 'Thames Path') and turn left. Pass to the left of the Adventure Dolphin Centre and enter Pangbourne Meadow. Bear right across the meadow to reach the River Thames. To your left you will see Whitchurch Bridge, one of the few toll bridges over the Thames. Turn right and follow the Thames until you reach a stone bridge over a stream.

2 Go over the footbridge, through a swing gate, then turn right with the stream on your right. On reaching the railway embankment, cross a stile on the right then turn left under the railway. Follow the track round a right-hand bend and in 30 yards turn left through a swing gate. With the stream once more on your right, continue ahead to reach the A329. Cross diagonally right and go along Sulham Lane opposite. Just before the road bends left through a small wood, look for a stile on the right.

3 Turn right over the stile, then bear slightly right across a field to reach, and go over, a stile and footbridge. Bear slightly left across the next field, passing to the right of a pylon. Go over a stile on the far side and again bear slightly left across a smaller field to reach the River Pang. Cross the river via the footbridge.

4 Ignoring a stile directly ahead, turn left on a path running between the river on your left and a wire fence on your right. After crossing a stile the path veers away from the river along the edge of a field. Go over a stile, beside a stable, and continue ahead to reach another stile, to the left of a six-bar gate. Cross this and turn right. In 5 yards turn left to join a drive. Go through a gate (note the red pedestal post box on the right) and continue ahead. Ignore the drive as it bends right and almost immediately, with the entrance to Longbridge directly ahead, turn right along an enclosed path, soon bending left. After crossing over a rough track the path bends right to emerge at the A340. Turn left to reach the thatched Greyhound pub.

5 Here, cross the A340 and go along Tidmarsh Lane opposite. Where the road bends left, turn right through a gate, signed 'Tidmarsh Farm', and follow an undulating track that meanders left, then right, along the field edge. Just after the sharp right turn keep to the left of a hedgerow to reach an enclosed path going left. Following a line of telegraph poles, the path eventually bends right and joins a gravelled drive leading out to a minor road. Cross the road and up the track opposite. Go through a gate and on past some old garages on the left, to reach a drive. Turn right to a drive junction. Here turn sharp left towards the buildings of Pangbourne College.

6 In 100 yards turn right down a drive, passing some tennis courts on the left, to reach a road, at a road junction. Cross with care, and turn left, taking the right-hand fork. Pass the entrance to Pangbourne College Junior House on the

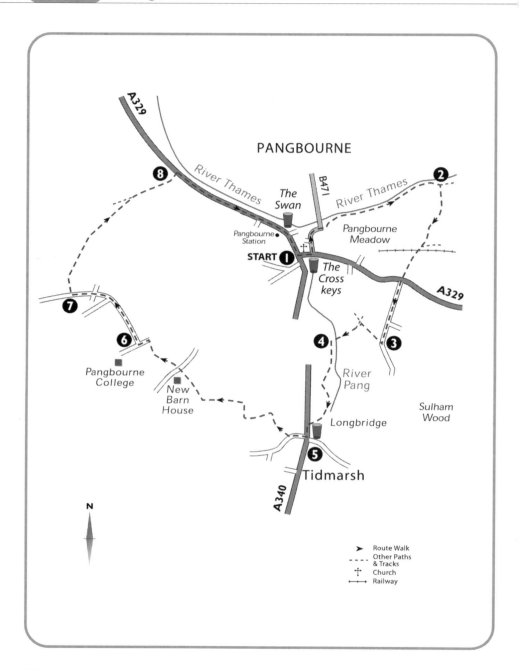

PANGBOURNE

River Thames

A329

The Swan

B471

River Thames

Pangbourne Station

Pangbourne Meadow

START ❶

The Cross keys

❽

❷

❼

❻

❹

❸

A329

River Pang

Pangbourne College

New Barn House

Longbridge

Sulham Wood

❺

Tidmarsh

A340

N

Route Walk
Other Paths & Tracks
Church
Railway

Taking a rest

left and in 20 yards turn right through a gap.

7 Head along the right-hand edge of a field and in the far corner bear right through a gap. Turn left and almost immediately bear diagonally right across a field, aiming to the left of a house. Continue along the right edge of the next field and in the far corner bear right through a swing gate. Now follow a meandering path down through Berry's Copse. At the bottom, pass through a tunnel under the railway to reach the A329.

8 Cross with care and turn right. With the River Thames on your left, follow the A329 into Pangbourne, passing the Swan on your left – this is reputed to be where 'Three Men in a Boat' ended their journey. Follow the road, under the railway, and back to the car park, which will be on the right.

Place of Interest
Beale Park is a nature theme park situated a few miles north-west of Pangbourne along the A329. Created by the philanthropist Gilbert Beale, in addition to the many varieties of birds there is a deer park; a willow maze and a miniature steam railway. Telephone: 0118 984 5172.

Date walk completed:

....

43

The George and Dragon

considering that the Blackwater, Whitewater and Loddon rivers flow nearby. This countryside walk, starting from the inn, takes you through part of the Swallowfield Park estate. King Charles II, Queen Anne, Charles Dickens and Charles Kingsley are all reputed to have stayed there. Using good paths and tracks the route crosses briefly into Hampshire and the longer walk takes you along the edges of Bramshill Plantation and Wellington Country Park before returning, via lanes and fields, to the inn.

S wallowfield is part of a large parish situated six miles south of Reading. Its name, derived from German, is said to mean 'rushing water' – very apt

Distance: *5 or 6¼ miles*

OS Explorer 159 Reading, Wokingham & Pangbourne
GR 736647

An easy walk on level ground

Starting point: The George and Dragon car park. Please obtain permission to leave your car while you walk. Alternatively, park in lay-bys around the village green.

How to get there: Approaching from junction 11 of the M4, take the A33 south. At the first roundabout turn left along the B3349, Basingstoke Road. After crossing the River Loddon turn left through Swallowfield, following the signs to Farley Hill. The George and Dragon is on the left, a short distance after crossing Salter's Bridge.

The **George and Dragon** has a cosy and smart interior behind its unassuming façade. Low wooden beams, stone-paved flooring, an open log fire in winter, and terracotta painted walls present a pleasing atmosphere. Beers include Brakspear Bitter, Wadworth 6X and Fuller's London Pride. Food, which is served by a young international staff, ranges from ciabatta with various fillings through to an à la carte menu. This is a very popular pub/restaurant and booking is recommended.

Opening times are 12 noon to 11 pm every day. Food is served from 12 noon to 2.30 pm and 7 pm to 9.30 pm.

Telephone: 0118 988 4432.

The Walk

1 Leave the car park and turn left. Immediately after passing the pub turn left to go through a gate and along a fenced path between fields. Pass a tree on the left and at a hedge corner continue ahead across the field. At the far side, turn right along the field edge and continue to the field corner. Here turn left through a gate. Looking left you have a distant view of Swallowfield House. In 10 yards turn right over a stile and continue ahead along a track to reach a road.

2 Turn right along the road. In 500 yards, at a byway sign, turn left along a hedged track. Ignore a path going left and continue ahead on the main track, bending right, to emerge at a road junction. Turn left and take the right-hand fork, Bungler's Hill. Follow it round a sharp right-hand bend and in 100 yards turn right at a bridleway sign.

3 Ignore a footpath on the left and continue along the bridleway as it bends sharp left. Being a bridleway it can get very muddy in places. On reaching a gate on the left bear slightly right to continue along the bridleway, which soon reaches a road, with Sandpit Farm to your right. Turn right along the road, passing the farm. Ignore a road going left and continue ahead, passing an electric substation on your right.

4 Just before reaching Wheeler's Farm turn left over a footbridge and stile and follow a fenced path around the field edge to reach the Blackwater River. Turn left along the bank of the river, taking in the peace and tranquillity of the countryside. Where the river bends right in a wide loop continue straight ahead to cross a bridge over the Blackwater River. Turn left, with the stream now on your left, to reach a stile and road. You are now in Hampshire.

5 *For the shorter walk turn right along the road – this follows the line of the old Roman road known as the 'Devil's Highway'. After, passing School Road on the right and a turning bearing left, you reach a crossroads. At this point (7) you rejoin the longer walk.*

For the longer walk, cross to the road opposite and in 20 yards turn left over a stile. With the river on your left, continue ahead along the field edge. At the far corner turn right, away from the river, again following the field edge before going through two gates to reach a road. Turn right along the road, with Bramshill Plantation on your left. At the road junction turn left to pass between some low wooden posts. Keeping the plantation on your left continue ahead on a bridleway for ½ mile. Shortly after passing Springwater Cottage on the right look for a bridleway on the right.

6 Here, turn right across the road and continue along a track, passing through a gate beside an old military bunker. Go through a second gate and, ignoring a path going left, cross a bridge over the Whitewater River. Follow an enclosed path to reach a wide service lane. Turn right here, passing The Miller's House on your right, to reach a road at a bend. Continue straight ahead along the road, with the boundary hedge and fence of Wellington Country Park on your left. At a fork bear left to reach a crossroads. Turn left.

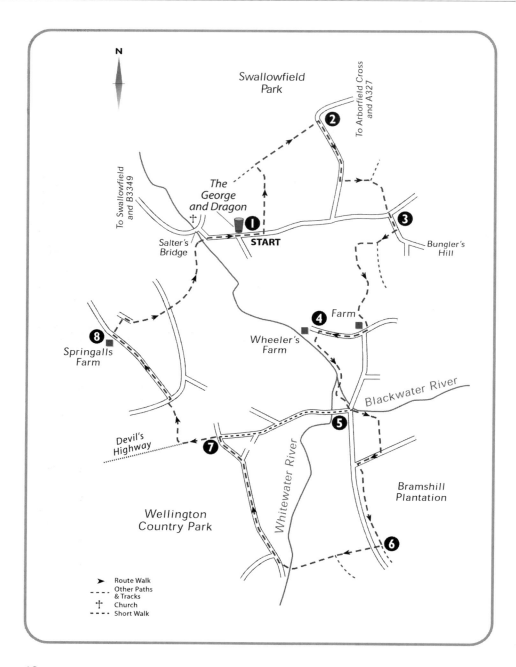

The River Whitewater, near the Berkshire/Hampshire border

7 Continue along the 'Devil's Highway'. Pass Christmas Cottage on the left and in 50 yards turn right over a plank bridge and stile. Go along the right-hand edge of a field then fork left to pass to the right of a tree, aiming to the right of some farm buildings, to reach a road. Turn right and in 30 yards turn left along Trowes Lane.

8 Just past Springalls Farm, on the left, turn right over a stile. Bear slightly left across the field. At the far side cross a stile and bridge and turn right along a fenced path, continuing along the edge of two fields to reach a road. Cross diagonally right to a path opposite. Bear left across a few fields, passing over some small stone bridges in between. On reaching the Blackwater River, go over a footbridge and along an enclosed path to reach a road. With Salter's Bridge just to your left, turn right and follow the road back to the inn.

Place of Interest
Wellington Country Park, part of the Duke of Wellington's estate, offers the family a number of attractions and activities ranging from nature trails, crazy golf, a miniature railway and a playground. There are also picnic sites and barbecue areas within the park. It is open between March and November. Telephone: 0118 932 6444.

Date walk completed:

....

47

Finchampstead

The Queen's Oak

This super walk starts from the Queen's Oak, near Finchampstead church, and takes in the woodland of Finchampstead Ridges before dropping down to the Blackwater Valley and the lakes of Moor Green Nature Reserve. The River Blackwater is followed to bring you to an area with royal connections. A plaque, near point 7 on the walk, reports an incident involving King Henry VII and his sons that took place in 1501 when they were hunting in the area.

The **Queen's Oak** obtained its current name from an oak tree that was planted on the green in 1897 in honour of Queen Victoria's Diamond Jubilee. With the Devil's Highway, the old Roman road that ran from Silchester to London, passing nearby it is thought that there may have been a hostelry here in Roman times. The present building is partly Tudor. The 16th century main door was once the porch door of St James's church. The pub's earlier name, the White Horse, is a reminder of the times when it was a coaching inn. There is a good stock of Brakspear ales, and food ranges from steak and ale pie to Cajun chicken, gammon or steaks. Children under 14 are welcome to use the garden but not the bars.

Opening times are 11 am to 3 pm on Monday to Saturday; 5.30 pm to 11 pm on Monday to Thursday and Saturday; 5 pm to 11 pm on Friday; 12 noon to 10.30 pm on Sunday. Food is served between 12 noon and 2 pm every day and from 6.30 pm to 9 pm on Monday to Saturday (not Sunday). A barbecue is often held during the summer months.

Telephone: 0118 973 4855.

Distance: *7 miles*

OS Explorer 159 Reading, Wokingham & Pangbourne
GR 793639

A fairly easy walk, with one relatively steep descent and one long gentle ascent near the finish

Starting point: The Queen's Oak car park. Please obtain permission to leave your car while you walk. Alternatively, park near the green or the church.

How to get there: Turn off the A321 south of Wokingham, taking the B3016 to Finchampstead. Before reaching the village take a turning on the right, signed 'To the Church'. The pub will be on the right.

The Walk

1 With the pub at your back, turn left down Church Lane. Immediately after passing Church Farm Bungalow turn left through a kissing gate and go diagonally right across a field. Go through a kissing gate in the far corner. Cross the B3016 road and turn left. In 10 yards turn right through another kissing gate and up the right-hand edge of a field. At the top continue ahead along an enclosed path, passing a barrier to reach a private road. Turn right, passing a house on your right, and descend on a narrow path to reach a metalled road. Turn left, passing Wick Vale Cottage on the right, to reach a T-junction.

2 Turn right here and follow Heath Ride for just over ½ mile.

3 At a junction, where the metalled drive bends left, turn right along a track leading into the woods. Go over a cross track, the Devil's Highway, and continue ahead with Heath Pond on your right. Go over another cross path and in 100 yards, where the open scrub on the right ends, turn left up a rutted track. Follow the track as it bends right and remain on it, ignoring all turns left and right, to reach the B3348. Cross, with care, and continue along the track opposite. Ignore a path going right and continue ahead for another 50 yards.

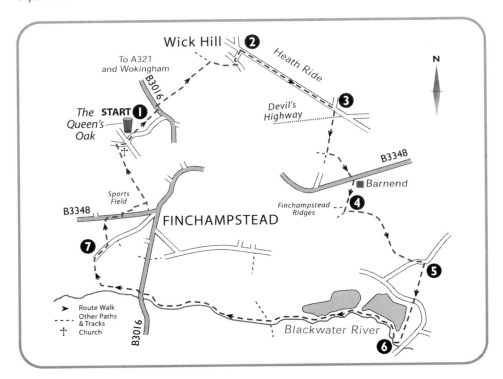

4 Just before the track starts to ascend steeply, turn left on a path that meanders through the trees. You are now on part of the Finchampstead Ridges. Depending on the amount of foliage on the trees you may get a glimpse of the view over the Blackwater Valley to the south. At the end of the wood, with a field ahead, the path bears right down a gully. Continue ahead between fields, then a field and wood, to reach a track. Turn left to reach a road. Ambarrow Farm is just opposite. Turn left along the road.

5 Just before the road bends sharp left, turn right through a kissing gate. Follow the right-hand edge of three fields to reach a lane. Cross the lane diagonally right to go over a footbridge and through two kissing gates opposite. Continue straight ahead, with a lake on your right. Pass to the right of the Water Sports Centre and as you approach the car park the path bends right over a bridge and along some duckboards. Ignore a gate and road to your left and continue ahead to reach the Blackwater River.

6 Turn right and follow the path that runs between the Blackwater River on your left and the Moor Green Lakes and Nature Reserve on your right. Ignore a stile on the right and continue ahead to later pass a bridge spanning the Blackwater River on the left. When the main path bends sharp right continue straight ahead over a small stream, still keeping the main river on your left. Just before reaching a Sewage Works the path forks right to reach a road. Cross diagonally right. Go through a kissing gate opposite and turn left, then right along the field edge. At the far side go through another kissing gate and turn right along a path. Go over a footbridge and, ignoring a path going left, continue ahead.

7 As you reach the first house on the left, turn left up an enclosed path. (*Before doing so go ahead for ten paces to read the plaque on the oak signpost ahead of you.*) The path emerges at a road. Cross the road and turn right. Just 20 yards beyond a telephone kiosk turn left into the sports field. Turn right and follow the field edge as it bends left, then right, to reach a footpath. Here turn left. The path, level at first, starts to ascend and, ignoring a path going off left, you come to a kissing gate leading into the churchyard of St James's church. Go through into the churchyard, up some steps, and keeping the church on your right exit through the third gate on your left. Turn right downhill and at the green swing left to return to the Queen's Oak.

+----------------------------------+
| **Date walk completed:** |
| |
| .... |
+----------------------------------+

Place of Interest

California Country Park, situated to the north of Finchampstead, contains 65 acres of woodland within which can be found many different species of trees, orchids and other interesting flora and fauna. The park also includes Longmoor Lake, now devoted to fishing and aquatic wildlife. An information centre is available where details can be obtained. Telephone: 0118 973 0028.

Hurst and Dinton Pastures 14

The Green Man

This enjoyable walk takes you through the village of Hurst, a name reputed to mean a wood. The village was once set in the heart of the Great Windsor Forest. The route passes the 11th century church of St Nicholas. On reaching the north-east corner of Dinton Pastures Country Park, a horseshoe route through the park provides an opportunity to see some of the flora and fauna that can be found in this attractive area. The River Loddon is then followed north to Whistley Bridge where

we leave the stream to return to the Green Man via fields and tracks.

The **Green Man** dates back to the turn of the 17th century when it is thought to have been an alehouse, much smaller than it is today. The history of the pub indicates that Brakspears became involved in 1646 although they did not start brewing their own beer until 1779. Some of the wooden beams in the oldest part of the building are thought to be over 1,000 years old. Brakspear ales are the principal beers sold and a good menu is available, including spicy Cajun chicken and Mexican beef chilli.

Opening times are 11 am to 3 pm and 5.30 pm to 11 pm on Monday to Saturday; 12 noon to 3.30 pm and 6.30 pm to 10.30 pm on Sunday. Food is served from 12 noon to 2.30 pm and 6.30 pm to 9.30 pm on Monday to Saturday; 12 noon to 3 pm and 7 pm to 9 pm on Sunday.

Telephone: 0118 934 2599.

Distance: *6 miles*

OS Explorer 159 Reading, Wokingham & Pangbourne
GR 800740

This is an easy walk, mainly on the level

Starting point: The Green Man car park, Hurst. Please obtain permission to leave your car while you are walking.

How to get there: Hurst is on the A321 between Twyford and Wokingham. If approaching via the M4, turn off at junction 10, taking the A329(M) south towards Bracknell, then the A329 into Wokingham. From there take the A321 north towards Twyford. Once in Hurst turn right into Hinton Road after passing Hurst Cricket Ground. The Green Man will be down on the right.

The Walk

1 Leave the pub car park and turn left along Hinton Road. At the road junction, cross the A321 (with care) then turn left. In 30 yards, turn right along School Road, passing a pond on your left. Just after passing the playground of St Nicholas' school, turn left over a stile. Cross the playing field to go through two gates on the opposite side. Now head for the far left-hand corner of the field; go through a five bar gate then turn right along Orchard Road.

2 At the road junction bear left up Church Hill. Just before the road bends sharp right, turn right, through a gate, to follow a path through the graveyard of St Nicholas' church. Go around the church to its main entrance; then turn left to the road. The buildings opposite, erected in 1664, once housed a hospital for the poor. The Castle Inn, up to your left, was formerly the church house. Turn right down the road. In 100 yards, turn left over a stile and along the left edge of a field. Cross a second stile, then bear diagonally right across the next field to reach a hedged track leading to a road. Turn right along the road. Where it swings right, with the entrance to Hatchgate Farm on the left, go straight ahead across a wooden bridge and stile. Bear slightly left across the field to reach a stile and road at the far side. Turn right and, at a grassy triangle, bear left over the grass, then cross the B3030 to go along Sandford Lane opposite towards the gates of Hurst Grove. Turn left here, still along Sandford Lane, for 300 yards.

3 Just before the entrance to Hurst Golf Club turn left at a footpath sign. In 40 yards turn right through a gap and cross the car park diagonally right. Cross over the entrance road and go through the Black Swan Sailing Club car park opposite. Follow the path between boat compounds, bending left, then right over a bridge to reach the edge of Black Swan Lake. You are now at the north-east corner of Dinton Pastures Country Park. Turn left along the path that runs beside the lake. On reaching a picnic area, a good spot to feed the ducks, bear left to reach a children's play area on the right. At the playground corner turn right.

4 *To visit the Information Centre for refreshments bear left over a bridge and follow the path round, or through a car park, to reach the Centre. To resume the walk, return to this point.*

Keeping the play area on your right, continue ahead on a well-defined path. After passing a notice board, continue ahead to reach a multi-signed board at a path junction. Take the left fork, signed to 'Tufty's Corner', and at the next junction continue ahead with the lake on your right. (The path going left takes you to Tufty's Corner.) At the next junction, ignore a bridge on the left and bear right. You will now have the River Loddon to your left and the lake on your right. Keep on the main path and continue to the next junction. Here turn left (signed 'Lavell's Lake') and follow the path round to reach Sandford Lane.

5 Cross the road diagonally right to the footpath opposite. Ignore all turns to the right and follow the path that runs alongside the River Loddon until you reach a tarmac road at Whistley Bridge. If open quarrying is still taking place you

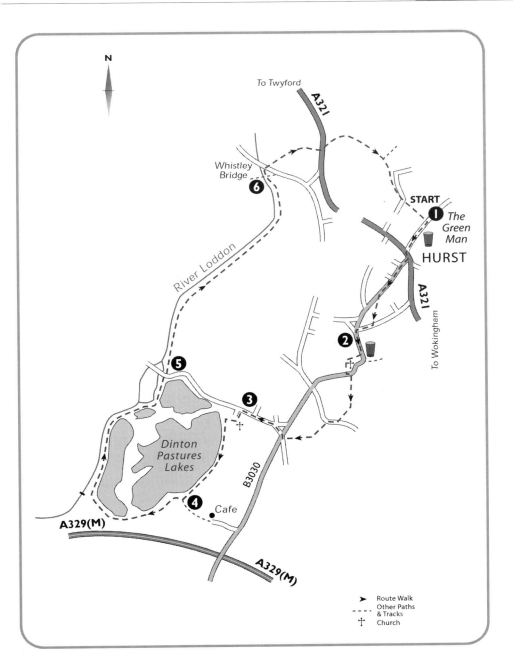

The River Loddon at Dinton Pastures

may have to cross over a quarry road and a gravel conveyer belt before you reach the road.

6 Turn right along the road and in 50 yards turn left along a fenced bridleway, running between fields. Ignore a path bending left and continue ahead to reach the A321. Cross, with care, to the bridleway opposite. Remain on the main track until you reach a road, on a bend. Continue straight ahead and after passing Little Farm on the right, turn right over a stile and immediately turn left along the field edge to cross a stile in the field corner. Cross the road to the stile opposite and then walk ahead across a small paddock to reach a stile and road. Directly opposite is the Green Man.

Cross the road diagonally right to return to the inn car park.

Place of Interest

Dinton Pastures Country Park covers an area of some 350 acres. The river meadows were once farmed by Anglo Saxons, who called the area Whistley, derived from the Saxon words *wisc*, meaning marsh meadows, and *lei*, meaning a wood clearing. The park has an Information Centre, a café and a number of self-guided trails. Telephone: 0118 934 2016.

Date walk completed:

....

Crazies Hill 15 Walk

The Horns

This scenic undulating route takes you over fields and along lanes to the outskirts of Wargrave before returning across further fields, and through woodland to Crazies Hill. Near the finish the route passes a small pictorial spring known as 'Rebecca's Well'. This was once the hamlet's main water supply.

The **Horns** is an attractive timber framed building, which is thought to have been a Tudor hunting lodge on the edge of the once extensive Great Windsor Forest. Adjoining the main bar is a 200 year old wood-beamed barn, now converted into a dining area. Sporting paintings and drawings adorn the walls of the bar, including one called 'cricket as played in 1743'. Brakspear Bitter and Special are the main ales available. There is a good choice of food on offer. Sunday roasts are very popular and you are advised to book in advance. There is a pleasant garden at the rear of the pub, where children are welcome.

Crazies Hill is a small hillside hamlet situated north-east of Wargrave. It obtained its name from the many buttercups, or crazies as they were once called, that grew in the surrounding fields.

Distance: *4½ miles*

OS Explorer 171 Chiltern Hills West GR 800809

A moderate walk across gently undulating countryside

Starting point: The Horns. Please obtain permission if you want to use the pub car park while you walk, otherwise park carefully elsewhere in the village.

How to get there: From the A4130 Henley to Maidenhead road at Remenham Hill take a minor road south to Cockpole Green. After passing two turnings going right, take a right hand fork then the first turning on the right. The Horns will be just on the right.

Opening times are 11.30 am to 2.30 pm and 6 pm to 11 pm on Monday to Saturday; on Sunday 12 noon to 6 pm all year plus 7 pm to 10.30 pm in the summer. Bar meals and restaurant times are from 12 noon to 2 pm every day and 7 pm to 9.30 pm on Monday to Saturday.

Telephone: 0118 940 1416.

The Walk

1 With your back to the Horns turn right along the road. Pass Crazies Hill C of E Primary School and in 100 yards turn right along a short enclosed path. Go over a stile and bear right across a small field. Crazies Hall, the white building seen over to the left, was once Henley's Town Hall. It was dismantled and moved to this site at the end of the 19th century. Go forward along the field edge for 20 yards and then fork left across the middle of two fields, aiming just to the left of a distant communications tower.

2 At the far side of the second field cross a stile and turn left along Worley's Lane, passing Worley's Farm on the left. Just before reaching a road junction at the bottom of a short hill bear left up a bank and through a swing gate. Now bear left along the field edge, keeping close to a wire fence on your left. At the top of the field continue straight ahead, now descending, to reach a squeeze stile and track (Penny Lane). Turn right and, almost immediately, turn left over a stile. Go up the left edge of a field and at the top bear left over a stile. A narrow path rises fairly steeply through scrub and woodland. Cross another stile at the top and bear right along the field edge. Keep just to the right of a farm track joining from the left, to reach a stile and road.

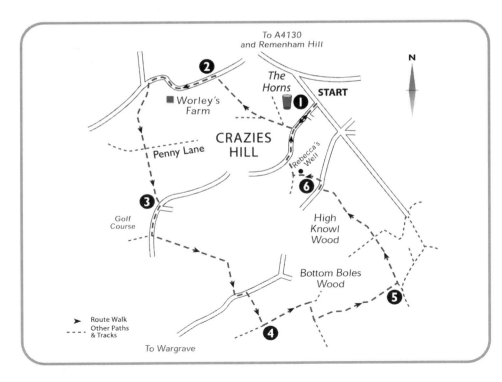

3 Turn right along the road, with Hennerton Golf Course on your right. In 200 yards turn left over a stile beside a gate and follow a path across the middle of a field. At the far side turn right along the field edge to reach a road. Turn left for 100 yards then turn right through a swing gate and follow the path along the field edge, with a ditch to your right.

4 At a path T-junction, turn left. Just before reaching the corner of a wood turn right over a stone bridge then immediately turn left to go along the edge of the wood, which will be on your left. Go over a stile in the corner and in 5 yards, at a path junction, turn right along a tree-lined bridleway. In 100 yards turn left at a stile and head along the right-hand edge of a field. At the far corner, bear right to go through a swing gate beside an iron rail. Continue straight ahead, crossing over a small gully. In 50 yards ignore a path bending left and cross the gully again on your right to go ahead up a path leaving the wood. Ascending gradually, ignore a stile on the right, and continue ascending into more woodland to reach a path junction.

5 Turn left downhill. The path meanders through the wood to reach another footpath junction. Here, go straight across and up the bank opposite. The path now meanders through a large clearing. At the far side ignore a path going off to the right and continue ahead, dropping down slightly to reach a wire fence on the right. Bear left, keeping the fence on your right, to reach a gate and road.

6 Go through a gap to the left of the gate then turn right along the road, around a

Rebecca's Well

sharp left-hand bend. As the road straightens, look for a bridleway on the left. Turn left here. The bridleway can get muddy in wet conditions. Look out for 'Rebecca's Well' on the right. The scene on the gabled cover over the well depicts a scene from the Book of Genesis, chapter 24. From the well continue ahead, ignoring a path going off left, to reach a road, with Rebecca's Cottage just on the right. Turn right uphill and follow the road back through Crazies Hill to return to the Horns, which will be on your left.

Place of Interest

Wargrave, or Weregrave as recorded in the Domesday Book, is a pleasant riverside village, mainly Edwardian in appearance. It attracts a fair number of boating enthusiasts and other visitors, especially during the summer. The daughter-in-law of Madam Tussaud, of waxworks fame, is buried in the churchyard of St Mary's church.

Date walk completed:

....

The Cricketers

Ivor Novello. Field and woodland paths take you over Ashley Hill, through the grounds of Hall Place, which today houses the Berkshire College of Agriculture, then on through Burchett's Green to Maidenhead Thicket, once the haunt of many a notorious highwayman. Here you have an opportunity to visit Robin Hood's Arbour, the site of an Iron Age enclosure, before returning to Littlewick Green.

This fascinating and interesting walk starts in the typically English village of Littlewick Green, once the home of the composer

Distance: 6 miles

OS Explorer 172 Chiltern Hills East and 160 Windsor, Weybridge & Bracknell GR 838800

Apart from the moderate ascent and descent of Ashley Hill, this walk is fairly level

Starting point: The Cricketers.

How to get there: Littlewick Green is just south of the A4, to the west of junction 9b of the A404(M). Approaching from the motorway, after negotiating a roundabout on the A4 take the second signed turning (Coronation Road) into Littlewick Green. The inn will be on the right, overlooking the village green.

The Cricketers was originally two separate cottages dating back to the late 19th century. A strong cricketing theme is to be found inside. Both the public and lounge bars are adorned with prints, paintings and photographs, all displaying aspects of this popular game. An old factory clock can also be seen in the lounge bar. Outside the front of the inn are some bench tables. Beers on offer include Badgers Best and Sussex Ale. Food is available every day and varies from sandwiches to game casserole and mushroom stroganoff. Sunday roasts are very popular.

Opening times are 12 noon to 3.30 pm and 5 pm to 11 pm on Monday to Friday; 12 noon to 11 pm at weekends (10.30 pm on Sunday). Lunch is served between 12 noon and 2 pm and dinner between 7 pm and 9 pm on Monday to Saturday; 12 noon to 3 pm on Sunday.

Telephone: 01628 822888.

The Walk

1 With your back to the inn turn left along Coronation Road. Just after a house called The Wilderness, 50 yards beyond the green, turn left along a narrow enclosed path. On emerging into a field continue straight ahead along the field edge. Approaching Frogmore Farm the path merges with a farm track. Go over a metalled farm road, along a short enclosed section, then across the middle of a field. Cross a stile at the far side into the car park at the rear of the Ring O Bells Inn. Pass to the left of the pub to reach the A4.

2 Cross the A4 (with care) to a footpath on the opposite side. Bear left through a wooded enclosure to the fence on the far side. Turn left and look for a gate stile in the fence on your right. Go over this and bear left across a field, aiming towards a distant gate. Just after passing a midfield telegraph post, turn right at a faint cross path and head towards Ashley Hill. Pass to the left of a small ringed enclosure to reach a gate at the field edge. Maintain direction across a track to a stile, at a signed multi-path junction.

3 Cross the stile and then bear right up the right-hand edge of two fields. Go

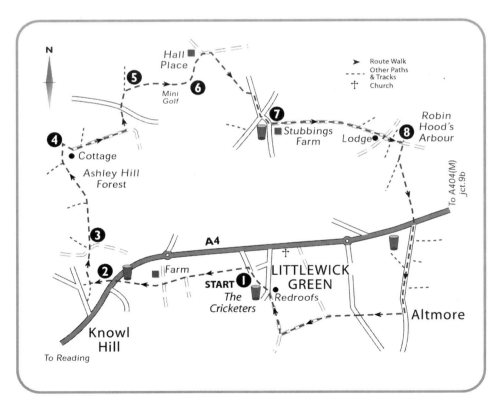

The old well at Littlewick Green

through a gate, just before the far corner, and maintain direction up the left-hand hedge of another field to reach a stile in the top left corner. Cross this and follow a meandering path up through Ashley Hill Forest. Go straight over a cross track, still ascending. At the top, ignore a path going left and continue ahead to pass to the left of a garden fence. Just beyond the fence the path descends to a footpath junction.

4 Turn right here to reach a drive, with the entrance to 'Clifton' on your right. Turn left down the drive. Just before the drive bends sharply to the right, turn left down a narrow path to reach a road. Cross the road and the stile opposite. Go along the right-hand edge of the field, for 150 yards, to reach a ladder stile on the right. Go over the stile. In 5 yards go

through a gate on the right and immediately turn left towards a pond.

5 Just before reaching the pond, turn left over a stile into an enclosed area. Follow the path round the pond and at the far side, bear right down the bank to reach the corner of another smaller pond, hidden in the bushes. Keeping this pond on your left, follow it round, over a small footbridge, to reach a stile beside a gate. Go over this and along the field edge. Go through a squeeze stile and ahead along the edge of a mini golf course to reach a track, with a sports field just beyond.

6 Turn left here. The track becomes metalled and bears right to reach the main drive of Hall Place, clearly visible in all its splendour on your left. Turn right along the drive. In 100 yards bear right to join a path going diagonally left across a field. At the far side, continue ahead to pass through a gate in the corner and along an enclosed path to reach a road. With Lane End House on the left, turn right along the lane to reach a road junction. Go straight over and along Burchett's Green Lane opposite, passing the Crown pub

❼ Where the road bends right, turn left through a gate and along a track, passing to the left of Stubbings Farm. At the far end, go over a stile and along a short enclosed section to reach and go over a second stile. Now follow the path through the middle of a tree-lined enclosure to reach a minor road. Cross this and bear left around a lodge to reach a signed path junction. Continue straight ahead along a fairly wide avenue. Go over a cross track to reach, in 40 yards, a second cross track. (*To visit Robin Hood's Arbour, an Iron Age enclosure dating back to pre-Roman times, continue ahead for another 100 yard, where there is a National Trust notice-board.*)

❽ Turn right along this track for about 200 yards then fork left, at a cross path. At the next junction fork left again and continue over two cross paths to reach the A4. Cross, with care, and go along Cherry Garden Lane opposite. At a house called Altmore, turn right along a cycle track. Cross a road and maintain direction along the track opposite. Where the track bends sharp left, turn right through a gate and follow a hedge-lined track. Where it merges with a road, continue straight ahead to reach the green. A plaque on Redroofs Theatre School wall, on the right, states that 'Ivor Novello (1893–1951) lived here'. Fork left at the green, passing an old well, to return to the Cricketers.

Date walk completed:

....

Places of Interest

Hall Place (Berkshire College of Agriculture). Although the building we see today dates from 1735, earliest records show that there was a manor house, known as La Halle, on the site in 1234. The current structure took seven years to build. Purchased by the Ministry of Agriculture in 1948, it became the Berkshire College of Agriculture in 1968. It is not open to the public but an open day is held in March every year.

Braywick Park and Nature Centre, Maidenhead. This can be found to the east of Littlewick Green, just off the A308 to Windsor. There is a designated nature trail and special events are held at the centre throughout the year. Tel. 01628 777440/796227 for details.

The Jolly Farmer

Thames, was also the home of artist Sir Stanley Spencer RA. His gallery in the village is well worth a visit. This delightful walk takes you down through Cookham Rise, along the edge of Cock Marsh close to the River Thames, before ascending to the top of Winter Hill. From here there are some fabulous views looking across the river towards the Chiltern Hills.

Cookham Dean was once the home of author Kenneth Grahame. It was the surrounding woods, and the Thames below Winter Hill, that provided the background and inspiration for his book, *The Wind in The Willows*. Cookham, nestling beside the River

The **Jolly Farmer** is a delightful village hostelry. Although parts of the building date back to the 18th century it did not become a pub until the late 19th century. A plaque near the entrance relates the fact that on 2 July 1987 the premises were 'bought by the village, for the village'. Real ales on offer include Brakspear Bitter, Young's Special and Courage Best. Bar meals include various sandwiches or you can try the Jolly Farmer's cod and chips. A separate dining area, which at one time was the local mortuary, offers an à la carte menu. There is an enclosed beer garden and children's play area at the back of the pub.

Distance: *4½ miles*

OS Explorer 172 Chiltern Hills East
GR 870851

A moderate walk with one gentle descent and one fairly steep ascent

Starting point: The Jolly Farmer. Please obtain permission if you want to leave your car in the pub car park while you walk. Roadside parking is available elsewhere in the village.

How to get there: From Maidenhead take the A308 north-west towards Marlow then turn right into Winter Hill Road (signposted 'Cookham Dean') and follow it into the village. The Jolly Farmer is on the left just before the church.

Opening times are 11.30 am to 11 pm on Monday to Saturday during the summer (April–September) and 11.30 am to 3 pm and 5.30 pm to 11 pm during the winter (October–March). Sunday opening is from 12 noon to 10.30 pm all year. Food is served between 12 noon and 2.30 pm (bar snacks available until 5 pm in summer) and from 7 pm until 9 pm. It is advisable to book if you intend using the dining area.

Telephone: 01628 482905.

The Walk

1 With your back to the pub turn left and in 20 yards, at a footpath sign, turn right. Pass to the right of St John's church and at the church wall corner turn left down a track, signed 'Sterlings Field'. Ignore a turning to the right and maintain direction downhill along a metalled track (Kennel Lane) passing Huntsmans Cottage. Go through a swing gate and continue downhill along an enclosed path. Ahead you can see the village of Cookham Rise and beyond that the rooftops of Cookham. The path emerges at a road, Whyteladies Lane. (*Guglielmo Marconi, the wireless communications pioneer, lived at number 142, in 1897, where it is thought he carried out some of his experimental transmissions.*) Cross the road and turn right. In 20 yards turn left into High Road. Pass Cookham Library on the right and follow the road round a left-hand bend. Go through Cookham station car park then turn right over the railway crossing. Continue along Station Hill to reach a road junction.

2 Here, turn left along Poundfield Lane. When the lane narrows continue ahead uphill, passing a house called Englefield on the right, to reach a road. Turn left uphill and in 20 yards bear right and almost immediately turn right down a narrow hedged path. Ahead you can see the River Thames as it makes a big loop around Cock Marsh, an open area that has been in the care of the National Trust since 1934.

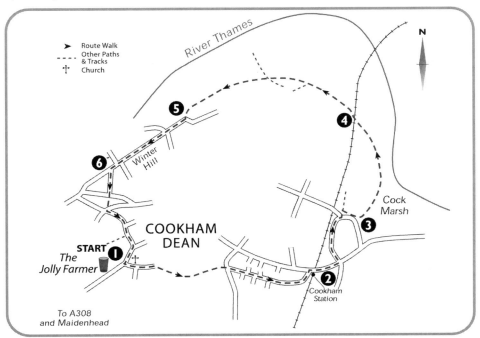

3 At the bottom go through a kissing gate and turn left. Soon a small stream joins on the right to run parallel with the path. At a footpath junction, where a stone bridge crosses the stream on the right, continue straight ahead on a permitted path. You now have a good view across Cock Marsh to the River Thames, and Bourne End on the opposite bank. The path skirts the edge of Winter Hill Golf Course on the left. Just after the fairway ends, go through a gate and turn left under the railway.

The view from Winter Hill

4 Immediately after passing under the arch, bear right through a kissing gate and continue ahead along the bottom of a steep slope. Ignore a footpath rising steeply up the slope on the left and carry on, staying at the base of the slope, until you reach a footpath junction. Just before the footpath sign bear left up a chalky track. As you ascend fairly steeply, good views start to open up across the River Thames over to your right. At the top go over a stone stile and continue ahead, ignoring all paths leading off left and right, to reach a road. A house called Chimneys is directly opposite.

5 Turn right along the road. At a road junction continue straight ahead, passing the Winter Hill National Trust sign. Just beyond the sign use a path on the right to take you up to the viewpoint. This is safer than walking along the road, which can get quite busy especially in summer. The panoramic view looking north across the Thames to the lakes and the southern slopes of the Chilterns beyond is well worth the effort you have made to reach this point. Having savoured the view, continue along the road, passing Startin's Lane on the left and Dial Place on the

right, and follow it as it bends left then right. In 150 yards, look for a bridleway sign on the left.

6 Turn left down Job's Lane. Go straight over Dean's Lane and continue down the path opposite. Cross over the next road and up the grassy bank opposite to reach a chalky track. Turn left up the track to reach the common. Continue straight ahead past the Inn on The Green pub sign and at the war memorial bear right along Church Road to return to the Jolly Farmer, which will be on the right.

Place of Interest
Stanley Spencer Gallery and Museum, High Street, Cookham contains a collection of his work, letters, documents and memorabilia, including a pram in which he used to carry his equipment when he went out to paint landscapes. A copy of his painting *The Last Supper* can be found in the nearby church. Telephone: 01628 471885.

Date walk completed:

The Golden Retriever

Swinley Forest, covering over 1,000 hectares, is the largest area of unbroken woodland in Berkshire. This enjoyable walk has much to offer in the way of interest in addition to the trees and plants seen along the way. The route, using good tracks throughout, visits Caesar's Camp, an Iron Age fort; passes Wickham Bushes, the site of an old Roman town; and takes in a short stretch of the Devil's Highway, the old Roman road that ran between Silchester and London. The walk starts from the car park at the Look Out Discovery Centre, where refreshments and information are available.

Distance: 5½ miles

OS Explorer 160 Windsor, Weybridge & Bracknell
GR 877661

This is a moderate walk using good tracks; the terrain within Swinley Forest is undulating

Starting point: The Look Out Discovery Centre car park. Please check on closing times as the gates are locked after dusk. It is possible to start the walk from the Golden Retriever but there are two busy roads to cross before entering Swinley Forest, near Caesar's Camp.

How to get there: From the A322 on the southern edge of Bracknell, turn westwards onto the B3430 to reach the Look Out, which will be on the left. To get to the Golden Retriever, continue along the B3430. The inn is on the left just beyond the next roundabout.

The **Golden Retriever** is a sparkling new pub/restaurant, opened fairly recently. Its modern décor is homely and comfortable and it is difficult to believe that the building has been developed from what was once boarding kennels (hence the name). The inn is divided into separate dining areas, smoking or non-smoking. There is a small garden at the front with bench tables and chairs and although situated close to the B3430, I did not find the traffic intrusive. Food varies from sandwiches through to a comprehensive mixed grill.

Opening times are 11.30 am to 11 pm on Monday to Saturday; 12 noon to 10.30 pm on Sunday. Food is available between 12 noon and 10 pm but sandwiches are only available until 5 pm on Monday to Saturday.

Telephone: 01344 868535.

The Walk

❶ Facing the Information Centre, pass to the left of the building, through a picnic area, to reach and go through a gate where there is a signpost. Take the track going diagonally right in the direction indicated by a Rambler's Route sign. Keep to the main track as it bends left. At a cross track continue straight ahead, now following Heritage Trail signs and discs. Ignore both a track on the right and, a short distance further on, a track veering off to the left.

❷ At the next cross track turn right, passing Forest Pond on your left to reach another cross track, halfway up a short sharp rise. Here, turn right. Where the main track bends right continue straight ahead down a narrow path, passing a sign indicating that the path is unsuitable for horses and cyclists. The fence on your left forms the boundary of Caesar's Camp. Pass a notice board on the left, just inside the fence, and 100 yards further on pass a gate leading into the enclosure. Continue ahead along the path, which eventually bends left with the Camp boundary, to reach a gate and stile.

❸ Cross the stile and in 5 yards bear left through a swing gate in the boundary fence of Caesar's Camp. Ascend fairly steeply up the bank of the hill fort. At the top continue ahead to reach a track junction. To your left, and slightly behind, is another information board. At the track junction continue straight ahead, ignoring all tracks going left and right, to

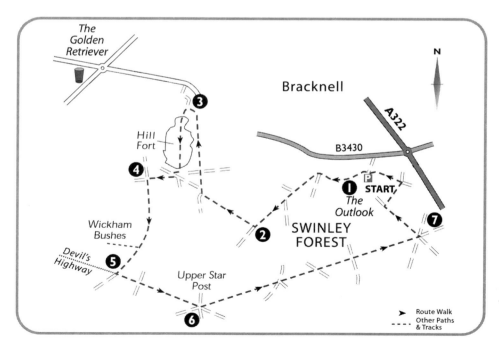

The entrance to the Look Out Discovery Centre

cross track is the old Roman road, known as the Devil's Highway.

5 Turn left through the gate and follow the Devil's Highway until you reach a multi-track junction – Upper Star Post. As you walk along the Highway take note how straight this thoroughfare is. Legend has it that no living being could build a road as straight as this and its construction was attributed to be the work of the Devil. Thus it was that it inherited its name.

reach the southern boundary fence. Go through a swing gate and immediately turn right. Pass a stile on your right and in 10 yards fork left down through an avenue of trees. At the bottom, pass between a couple of posts to reach a cross track.

4 Here, turn left and follow a well-defined track for approximately ½ mile. To your right you will pass an area known as Wickham Bushes. The area is not very clear or easily defined, but it was once the site of a small Roman town. Further along, at a track going off to the right, there is a convenient bench seat where you can rest your weary legs. Ignoring the track on the right, continue straight ahead until you reach a cross track, with a large gate to your left. This

6 At the Upper Star Post junction take the second track bearing slightly left, signed to the Look Out and Pudding Hill. Ignore three tracks going left and at the next track junction, continue straight ahead towards Pudding Hill. Go over two further cross tracks to reach another multi-track junction.

7 Here, turn left, following the direction of the Look Out fingerpost. At the first track going right, turn right. At the next cross track, turn left, passing a treetop rope assault course on your right, to reach a gate leading into the Look Out car park area.

Date walk completed:

....

Places of Interest
The Look Out Discovery Centre includes numerous science and nature exhibits and many other attractions for the family. There are also several waymarked walks and you can try out your navigational skills on one of the permanent orienteering courses. Telephone: 01344 354400.

Caesar's Camp is the site of an Iron Age hill fort. The enclosure covers an area of about 20 acres in size. Information boards have been erected at strategic points, relating the history of the fort and showing what it may have looked like during that period.

The Rose and Crown

Mention the word Ascot and thoughts of the pomp and ceremony of Royal Ascot quickly spring to mind. This delightful walk presents an opportunity for you to walk across this world famous racecourse, a venue first initiated by Queen Anne in 1711. If racing is taking place you may have to wait before you can cross. Before reaching the racecourse the route meanders through part of Windsor Forest, passing a large tranquil lake hidden amongst the trees in Sunninghill Park. Although the return involves some road walking, it does take in a section of an old coach drive that once led to Ascot Place.

The **Rose and Crown** is an attractive, welcoming 200 year old pub. The bar and non-smoking dining area have low wood-beamed ceilings and the walls are decked with horse racing paintings, which is not surprising considering the close proximity to Ascot Racecourse. A side garden has tables and chairs and there is a set of swings for children. A good selection of food, ranging from sandwiches to steaks, is available. The beer includes Greene King IPA, Morland Original and a guest ale.

Opening times are 11 am to 11 pm on Monday to Saturday; 12 noon to 7 pm on Sunday. Food is available from 12 noon to 2.30 pm on Monday to Saturday and from 7 pm to 9.30 pm on Tuesday to Saturday. Sunday lunch is served from 12 noon to 4 pm.

Telephone: 01344 882051.

Distance: *6 miles*

OS Explorer 160 Windsor, Weybridge & Bracknell
GR 928710

An easy walk on fairly level ground

Starting point: The Rose and Crown car park. Please obtain permission to leave your car while you walk.

How to get there: Woodside is situated just off the A332 between Windsor and Ascot. Coming from Windsor, take the first turning on the right after passing the Crispin pub. From the south, pass the junction with the A330 and turn left. Turn right again into Woodside Road. The inn is about 100 yards on the right.

The Walk

1 Leave the pub car park and turn right along Woodside Road. At the road junction turn right, passing Woodside Lane on the left. In 200 yards turn right along a short track that runs behind the Crispin pub. Cross the A332 diagonally right (with care) to a track opposite, signed 'Woodend Cottages'. Pass to the left of the cottages and continue ahead over a cross track, passing a sign that reads 'Horses prohibited'. Follow the path as it meanders through woodland. At the next cross track (Strood Lane), go straight across, through squeeze stiles either side. Bear slightly right across a field to a stile, just to the left of a metal gate, on the far side. Continue ahead on a wide track up through Paddock

Wood and remain on it as it bends left to reach a metalled drive and a corner of the Great Pond. Cross the drive to a path directly opposite. The path meanders gently down though woodland. Cross a footbridge, over a small stream, and then bear left uphill to reach a minor road.

2 Turn right uphill to a road junction. Turn right here along Cheapside Road. The Royal Family use the first set of white gates you pass on the right during Royal Ascot week. At the next road junction bear right along New Mile Road. A section of Ascot Racecourse, the original long mile, can be seen up to your right. Ahead is the main racecourse.

3 On reaching the A330, turn right and

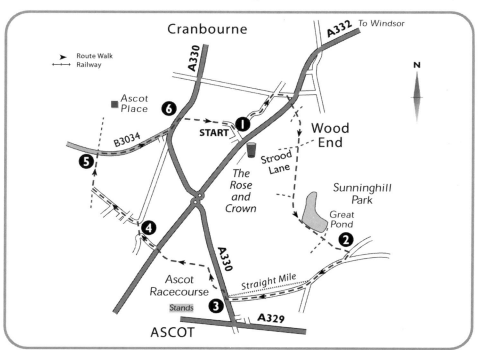

immediately after crossing the long mile, turn left to pass between some small white posts. In 20 yards bear diagonally right, with Royal Ascot Golf Clubhouse on your right, to reach a gate at the corner of the car park. Go though the gate and follow a clear track across the racetrack. At the far side turn right along a service road just inside the racetrack. In 200 yards go diagonally left on the narrower tarmac drive. Pass the cricket pavilion on the right to reach the far side of the racecourse. At this point note the rails in the ground on your right. These are to enable a section of the turf to be moved away from the course; thus enabling transport to come onto the heath without crossing the grass. This was installed in October 2000 and was the first of its kind in the world. Cross the course and through the gate to the A332. Cross with care and go along Kennel Avenue opposite. At the far end follow the road round to the right.

4 In 100 yards, at a house called Huntsman Meadow on the right, turn left across the road to a narrow enclosed path opposite. On reaching a road turn left. At a mini roundabout, with New Road going off right, continue straight ahead, passing the Royal Hunt pub on the left. At the next mini roundabout, carry straight on along Rhododendron Walk. At the far end go through a gate and turn right along the old coach road to reach the B3034. Cross with care to the pavement opposite.

5 Turn right to reach the junction with the A330. Here, bear left along Hatchet Lane.

6 In 150 yards, just after passing the

Ascot racecourse

Cranbourne sign, cross the road, with care, to go along Hodge Lane opposite. When the metal surfaced drive bends right into Downy Field continue straight ahead along a tree-lined track. When the track becomes metalled bear left and immediately right to reach the Duke of Edinburgh pub, on the corner of Woodside Road. Turn left here to return to the Rose and Crown.

Place of Interest

Legoland, situated on the B3022 Windsor to Ascot road, is a theme park providing over 50 different activities within its 150 acres. There are various types of rides, mazes, theatres, cafés and restaurants. It is open between March and October and in addition to its permanent activities it also holds special events both in and out of season. It provides a good family day out and caters for grandmas and grandpas as well as for parents and children. There is also a park and ride facility for those wishing to visit nearby Windsor. Telephone: 01753 743900.

Date walk completed:

....

The Union Inn

has to be the section of Windsor Great Park that the route passes through. The Deer Park, Rhododendron Drive, the Royal Lodge, the Copper Horse and the Long Walk, with excellent views of Windsor Castle, are all featured. And why not take the opportunity to visit the world famous Savill Garden when you pass? The seasonal blossoms will bring you back time and again.

Old Windsor has a history that predates modern day Windsor. At the time of the Domesday Book it was the third largest settlement in Berkshire. Although this picturesque walk starts in Old Windsor the highlight

Distance: 6 miles

OS Explorer 160 Windsor, Weybridge & Bracknell
GR 980740

An easy walk with a few gentle undulations

Starting point: The Union Inn. Please obtain permission if you want to use the inn's car park, which is at the rear of the pub, while you walk.

How to get there: Old Windsor is on the A308 between Staines and Windsor. Turn south off the A308 at the Windsor end of the village into St Mark's Road, then fork right into Crimp Hill. The Union Inn will be on the right.

The Union Inn got its name from the old Union Workhouse that once existed nearby. Luxury houses stand on that site today. The inn itself has a pleasant, friendly atmosphere and photographs of show business celebrities adorn the walls. Two of its previous landlords were ex Chelsea footballers Peter Osgood and Ian Richardson. Hanging from the black wooden beams above the bar is a splendid collection of old currency notes. The choice of food ranges from hot and cold bar snacks to a more substantial à la carte or table d'hôte menu available in the separate Copper Pot Restaurant area. Beers include Theakston Best and Courage Best.

Opening times are 11 am to 11 pm on Monday to Saturday; 12 noon to 10.30 pm on Sunday. Food is served from 12 noon to 2.30 pm (Sunday 12 noon to 3 pm) and from 7 pm to 10 pm every day.

Telephone: 01753 861955.

The Walk

1 With your back to the inn, turn right along Crimp Hill, passing St Peter's School on your right. At a sharp left-hand bend, and just before a chevron sign, bear right past the entrance to Crimp Hill Cemetery. In 200 yards go through Bears Rails Gate and continue ahead to reach and go through a second gate into the Deer Park. Follow the track as it bends left away from the fence. The enclosed Bears Rails Scouts Campsite is just ahead of you on the right.

2 At the track junction fork left. The right-hand track leads into the campsite. The track ascends gently through woodland to reach a cross track. Go straight across and continue ahead uphill, ascending more steeply now. As you approach the Deer Park fence keep to the track as it bends right. When the fence veers left leave the track and cut across the grass to reach a metalled road. Turn left to go through the gate. The entrance to the Royal Lodge, once the home of the late Queen Mother, can be seen on the right. In 10 yards turn left. Keeping the Deer Park fence on your left head towards the Bishopsgate entrance into the park.

3 Just before Bishopsgate, near a wooden kiosk, turn right across the road. (Do not go out through the gate.) Pass the lodge, which will now be on your left, and almost immediately after passing the lodge garage, bear left through a green gate. Note the sign: 'To the Savill Garden'. Keep to the main track, ignoring any turnings veering off to the left. This track, enclosed by rhododendron bushes, is a mass of colour during May. Further along, through a gap on the right, Cow

Pond comes into view. This again, in season, is covered with a large number of colourful water lilies. Maintain direction, ignoring a path on the right going round the pond, and when a metalled track joins from the right continue straight ahead. Soon after you have passed the entrance to the Savill Garden, on the right, the obelisk comes into view.

4 Just before the monument make a sharp right turn, passing between the obelisk and the Savill Garden fence, and follow a wide path downhill. With the Savill Garden on the right and the Obelisk Pond on the left, go over a Palladian style bridge and continue up a wide grassy ride, aiming for a distant red brick building (Cumberland Gate Lodge). To your left, if you look back, are the Windsor Polo playing fields. On reaching a road turn right through Cumberland Gate. In 50 yards turn left on a track that bends left towards the rear of the lodge. In 20 yards look for a faint track on the right, meandering through the trees. If in doubt veer left to join a sandy bridleway that runs parallel with the path.

5 On reaching a drive, turn left towards Cumberland Lodge and in 20 yards bear right on a path that passes just to the right of some tennis courts. On reaching another drive turn right to a multi-drive junction. Here, turn left and in 20 yards, just before the entrance to Chaplain's Lodge, turn right on a path that soon descends between a fence on the right and Ox Pond on the left. At the bottom continue ahead along a wide, hedged ride. The Royal Lodge can be seen over to your right. On the rise ahead is the Copper Horse. Pass through the gate back into the Deer Park and maintain direction

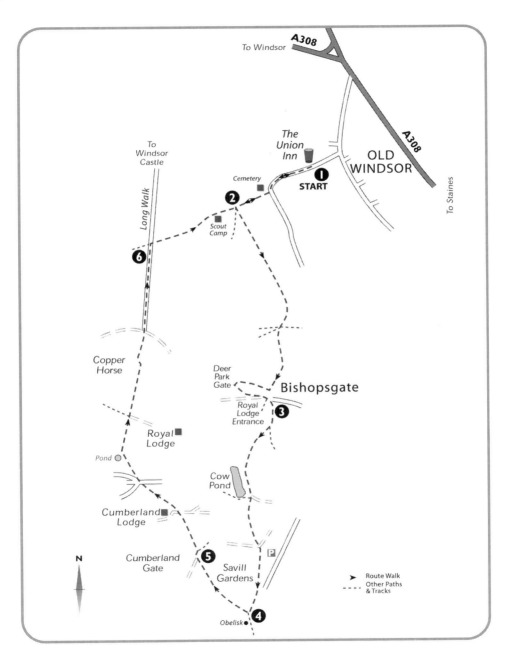

To Windsor **A308**

A308

The
Union
Inn

OLD
WINDSOR

To Staines

To
Windsor
Castle

Cemetery

Long Walk

START

❶

❷

Scout
Camp

❻

Copper
Horse

Deer
Park
Gate

Bishopsgate

Royal
Lodge
Entrance

❸

Royal
Lodge

Pond

Cow
Pond

Cumberland
Lodge

P

N

Cumberland
Gate

❺

Savill
Gardens

Route Walk
Other Paths
& Tracks

Obelisk

❹

73

The Copper Horse in Windsor Great Park

up to the statue. You are now standing on the summit of Snow Hill, the highest point in the park. On a clear day you can see the planes take off from Heathrow Airport. From the statue head down the slope and join the Long Walk, heading straight towards Windsor Castle, 2½ miles away.

6 In ½ mile, where a track crosses the Long Walk, turn right through the avenue of trees and then veer left towards a fence. Keeping the fence on the left, continue ahead to pass Bears Rails Pond and Scout Campsite on your right. Veer left with the fence and go though the Deer Fence gate to retrace your steps back to the Union Inn – through the second gate, ahead along the lane, then left at the road junction.

Date walk completed:

....

Places of Interest

The **Savill Garden**, originally developed by Sir Eric Savill in 1932, is open every day except Christmas Day and Boxing Day. A garden for all seasons, it has a coffee shop, restaurant, gift shop and planteria. Telephone: 01753 847518.

Windsor Castle has a history spanning more than 900 years. It is the world's largest and oldest inhabited castle. It is open all year round although opening arrangements for either whole or parts of the castle are subject to change at short notice. Details of opening times can be obtained either by phone – 020 7766 7304 – or at www.windsor.gov.uk or www.royal.gov.uk

The Bell Inn

green, attractive cottages and 12th century church, the longer circuit leads you across farmland to the village of Epwell. There are good views of the three hills, Epwell Hill, Yarn Hill and Rough Hill, that are situated just to the north of the village. From Epwell the route back to Shenington follows the shared D'Arcy Dalton Way and Macmillan Way, passing between two of the hills.

This attractive walk takes you into the remote but picturesque countryside of north-west Oxfordshire. Starting from the Cotswold hilltop village of Shenington, with its inn,

Distance: *3 or 5 miles*

OS Explorer 191 Banbury, Bicester & Chipping Norton
GR 371428

A moderate walk in gently undulating countryside, which includes a few short steep slopes

Starting point: The Bell Inn. Some parking is available around the village green or on the roadside elsewhere in the village.

How to get there: Turn off the A422 Banbury to Stratford-upon-Avon road at Wroxton Heath, 4½ miles west of Banbury, going south-west on a minor road signposted to Alkerton and Shenington.

The **Bell Inn**, reputed to be over 300 years old, has wooden beams, a flagstone floor and there is an open fire blazing during the cold winter months. During the summer you can sit out on the benched tables overlooking the green. It has a relaxed atmosphere and provides home-cooked food prepared using local produce. Children are welcome and dogs are allowed. Beers include Hook Norton Best and Flowers. Overnight accommodation is also available at the inn.

Opening times are 12 noon to 2.30 pm and 7 pm to 11 pm except on Mondays when the inn is closed. Bar and restaurant meals are available from 12 noon to 2 pm and 7 pm to 11 pm. It is advisable to book at weekends.

Telephone: 01295 670274.

The Walk

1 Facing the inn, turn left to the main road. Turn right up the road, passing Stocking Lane on the right, to reach Mill Lane on the opposite side. Turn left along Mill Lane, which, after passing a barn, becomes a farm track. There are good views of the undulating countryside ahead of you. Pass through two gates and gradually descend into a small valley to go through another gate into a field. Keep to the right-hand edge of the field and follow the hedge round to the right, to reach a footbridge and gate on the right.

2 Go through the gate and bear left up the middle of a field, passing just to the right of a pylon. Go through a gate at the top and maintain direction across the next field, heading towards a field barn. Pass to the left of the barn and then bear left along a track running along the field edge. At the field corner, keep to the track as it bends right through a gap into the next field. With a hedge now on your left continue ahead along the track. Ahead you can see Epwell Hill, Yarn Hill and Rough Hill. Where the track bends sharp left to Epwell Grounds Farm, continue straight ahead across the field. At the far side, go through a gate, over a farm track, and through the gate opposite. Now bear left across the field, aiming just to the left of a tall tree at the far side. Go over a stile and head towards a white

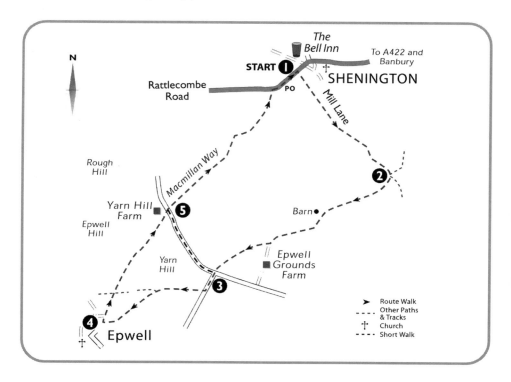

road sign at the far side of the next field, to reach a road.

3 *For the shorter walk, turn right along the road. Just after passing an electricity substation on the right look for a footpath sign on the right. Here you rejoin the longer route at point 5.*

For the longer walk, cross the road, with care, and continue along Epwell Road opposite. In 200 yards, turn right at a footpath sign (Epwell ½). Bear left for 30 yards then swing right around some small trees. Head across the field towards the left-hand edge of a hedgerow on the far side. Go through a gap, then bear right along the field edge, with a hedge on your right. Ahead, to your left, you can see the village of Epwell. Swing left at the far corner and, at the next field corner, go through a gap and along the edge of the next field to reach a footbridge and stile. Cross these and bear right, passing a house and garden on the right to reach a road. (*To visit Epwell turn left.*)

4 Turn right along the road, passing to the right of a small green, to reach a gate leading into private property. A footpath sign (Shenington 1¾) indicates this is a right of way. Go though the gate, along the drive, and where this bends right go straight ahead across the garden, following the direction of a D'Arcy Dalton Way disc. Go over a stile in the

far corner of a small meadow. The path now keeps to the left-hand edge of four fields, passing between Yarn Hill on the right and Epwell Hill on the left, before it emerges at a road. Turn left along the road for 30 yards to reach a footpath sign (Shenington 1) on the right.

5 Cross over the stile and bear slightly left across the field towards some solitary trees. Pass to the right of a telegraph pole and continue down a slope to reach a stile and footbridge. Cross these, then bear right up a steep slope to a stile at the top. Maintain direction across the next field, aiming just to the right of a distant barn. Drop down to a stile in the far corner and then bear right past an old footbridge, following the D'Arcy Dalton Way round the base of a small hill before dropping down to a gap in the bottom left-hand corner of the field. Go through the gap and bear slightly right up a steep slope to reach a gate at the top. Go through and head along the right-hand edge of a field. Cross a stile and bear half-left down another steep slope to a footbridge and stile, just to the left of a line of trees. Continue up the edge of the next field to reach a stile and road. Turn right and follow the road back into Shenington. The green and the Bell Inn will be on your left.

Date walk completed:

....

Place of Interest
Upton House is a late 17th century house with significant art collections and superb terraced gardens, including an interesting 1930s' water garden. The property is administered by the National Trust and is open on specific days of the week between April and October. It is situated on the A422, just north of Shenington. Telephone: 01295 670266.

The Blinking Owl Inn

Starting from the attractive village of North Newington this is an interesting countryside walk. It passes through an area of scrubland known as the Bretch from where it is said that, during the Civil War, a tunnel ran to Broughton Castle. The route also follows part of the Salt Way, an ancient thoroughfare that was used to transport salt from Droitwich to London. The walk then loops back to Broughton, where it enters Broughton Park, passing close to Broughton Castle. The house and grounds have been used as locations in a number of films, including *Shakespeare in Love.*

The **Blinking Owl Inn** dates back to 1645. It obtained its name when the then landlord, after being disturbed, made the comment 'It's that blinking owl again'. The barn, where the owl once made its home, has been converted into a restaurant area on the ground floor, and B&B accommodation on the first floor. The quaint narrow main bar has a wooden dresser adorned with a fine collection of owls. Beers available include John Smith's, Vale Best Bitter and Wells Bombardier. Food ranges from sandwiches through to steaks and chicken tikka. Vegetarians are also catered for.

Opening times are 12 noon to 2.30 pm and 6.15 pm to 11 pm (10.30 pm on Sundays). Food is available from 12 noon until 2 pm on Tuesday to Sunday and from 6.30 pm to 10 pm every day.

Telephone: 01295 730650.

Distance: *5½ miles*

OS Explorer 191 Banbury, Bicester & Chipping Norton
GR 419398

A moderate walk through undulating countryside

Starting point: The Blinking Owl Inn. Please obtain permission if you want to use the inn car park while you walk. Some roadside parking is available in the lay-by opposite the pub.

How to get there: Turn westwards off the B4035 south-west of Banbury just north of the village of Broughton. The inn is in the centre of North Newington.

The Walk

1 With your back to the Blinking Owl Inn, cross the road and go over the green opposite. Turn right along School Lane, passing Bishop Carpenter School on the left. As you approach the far end of the lane note the old water pump on the left. At the end of the lane, bear left up a drive and immediately after passing the entrance to Tiggs Court, turn right, with a hedge on your right. Go over a stile and head down the left-hand edge of a field to a stile in the far corner. Cross this and turn right along the edge of another field. At the far corner, cross over two concrete bridges and continue ahead along the left-hand edge of a field to reach a small plantation. Turn right up the field edge, keeping the plantation on your left.

2 At the top corner of the field, turn left through a gap in the top edge of the plantation and then continue ahead along the field edge, with a hedge on your right. The path, level at first, drops down to meet a cross path in the far corner. Here, turn left. In 20 yards, turn right by a wooden post. Go down a few steps and straight across an open area to a track directly opposite. Follow the track for 20 yards then bear right down a bank to join a narrow path meandering through the bushes and trees of the Bretch. The path brings you to a footbridge and steps leading up to a road (B4035)

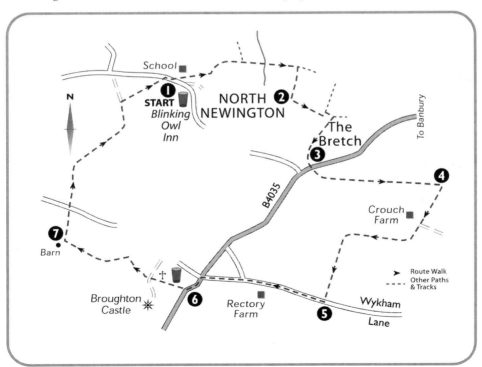

3 Cross the B4035 (with care) then bear right along the right of way (the Salt Way) opposite. The gravelled track swings sharply left and continues between bushes and trees. In approximately ½ mile look out for the buildings of Crouch Farm behind the hedge on your right (the farm is not always easy to see). Continue for another 150 yards and look for a gap in the hedge on your right.

4 Turn right through the gap, over a footbridge, and bear half-right across two fields, aiming towards the left-hand corner of the farm buildings. Here, turn left, with a fence and the farm on your right. Go over a concrete drive and along a track running parallel with the right-hand field boundary. At the far right-hand corner, turn right through a gate. In 40 yards, turn left through a gap in the hedge and immediately turn right along the field edge. At the far corner, go through a gate and turn left along the field edge until you reach a road.

5 Turn right along Wykham Lane. As you enter Broughton village, ignore the main road going off right and continue ahead to reach the junction with the B4035. Cross the road, with care, and turn left down the B4035, passing the Saye and Sele Arms.

6 In 200 yards turn right along a walled path leading over Sor Brook to Broughton church. Go through the churchyard, keeping to the left of the church, and out through the far gate into Broughton Park. With the entrance to Broughton Castle to your left, continue directly ahead along a drive leading away from the church. Where this bends right, carry straight on across the grass. In 100 yards, bear left towards a fairly large copse at the top of the hill. Pass to the right of the copse to a stile in the fence ahead. Cross the middle of a field towards a barn at the far side.

7 Pass to the right of the barn to join a track. Go through a gate and follow the track up the edge of a field to reach a road. Cross the road to a footpath just opposite (signed 'North Newington ¾'). Walk up the right-hand edge of the field, through a gate in the top corner and along the edge of the next field. Go through another gate at the top then bear half-left across the next field. At the opposite corner, turn left through a gap and walk ahead, keeping a hedge on your right. In 40 yards, turn right through a gap in the hedge and immediately turn left. In 30 yards, bear right across the field. At the far side, go through a gap to reach a track. Turn left, past Pound Cottage, to reach Main Street. Turn right to return to the Blinking Owl Inn.

Place of Interest

Broughton Castle was built as a fortified manor house during the 14th century. In the 15th century it passed, through marriage, into the hands of William Fiennes, the 2nd Lord Saye and Sele. The castle has remained with the Fiennes family ever since. It had close connections with the Civil War period, when meetings were held there. Open between 2 pm and 5 pm on specific days between May and September. Telephone: 01295 276070.

Date walk completed:

....

Salford and the Rollright Stones 23

The Black Horse

Starting from the ancient village of Salford, west of Chipping Norton, this walk takes you through rolling countryside near the Oxfordshire/Warwickshire border. The route passes close to the Rollright Stones, which are thought to date from about 2500–2000 BC. They consist of three main features, the Whispering Knights, the King's Men stone circle and the King Stone; the latter is actually in Warwickshire. There is a good view of Chipping Norton on the return leg of the walk.

The **Black Horse** dates from the late 17th century. There is some wood panelling in the main bar and old photographs of the village adorn the walls. The inn has a pool table. There is a pleasant garden at the rear, including an 'Aunt Sally' pitch. The game is very popular in this area. The inn has a small car park. Beers include Hook Norton Best and Flowers Best. Food includes sandwiches and cooked meals.

Opening times are 11 am to 3 pm daily and 6 pm to 11 pm on Monday to Saturday; 7 pm to 10.30 pm on Sunday. Food is available from 12 noon until 2 pm daily. Evening meals are available if ordered in advance.

Telephone: 01608 642824.

Distance: 7¼ miles (add ¾ mile to visit the stone circle)

OS Explorer 191 Banbury, Bicester & Chipping Norton
GR 288279

A moderate walk through undulating countryside

Starting point: The Black Horse. Please seek permission from the landlord if you want to use the pub car park while you walk. Some parking is also available in the village hall car park.

How to get there: Salford is about 1½ miles to the west of Chipping Norton on the A44 Moreton-in-Marsh road. The pub is just off the main road.

The Walk

1 Leave the pub car park and turn right. At the T-junction, turn right. In 30 yards, with the village hall on the left, turn left up Cooks Lane. At the top follow the road round a right-hand bend. Pass a playground on the right, and at the road junction, turn left along a lane, passing a sign stating 'Trout lakes – Rectory Farm'. At a track leading off left, turn left (signed 'D'Arcy Dalton Way').

2 In 20 yards turn right, through some trees, to a stile. Cross the field beyond, aiming just to the left of a barn at Rectory Farm. Go over two stiles and ahead along the right-hand hedge of a field. Where the hedge on the right bends right continue straight ahead to reach a stile. Cross this and then follow a narrow path through the trees. Go through a gate at the far end and along the edge of a field. At the far corner, go through a gate on the right and immediately turn left along the field edge, with a hedge on your left. At the field corner, go straight ahead to cross a small stream and stile. Go over a farm track and into the woodland opposite. Now follow a meandering path, gradually ascending through the wood. At the top go through a gate and head along the left-hand edge of a field. There are excellent views to your right. Go through a gap, just to the right of the far corner and then maintain direction across the middle of a field towards some farm buildings (Manor Farm), almost hidden in the small valley ahead. Pass between two barns, across a yard, and up a drive to reach a minor road.

3 Turn left for 30 yards, then turn right up a field, still following the D'Arcy

Dalton Way signs, to reach a road. Cross the road and go through the gate opposite. The path runs between fields to reach a stile, almost hidden in the hedge. Before you reach the stile the Whispering Knights can be seen over to your left.

4 *To visit the Whispering Knights, do not cross the stile but turn left along the field edge. To visit the other stones, continue ahead to the road and turn left. The King Stone will be in a field to your right and further on you reach an entrance on your left leading to the King's Men stone circle. To continue the walk, retrace your steps to the stile mentioned above.*

Go over two stiles and ahead through a small plantation. Cross a stile on the far side and turn right down a track, leaving the D'Arcy Dalton Way. Pass to the left of Brighthill Farm, over a stile and then bear diagonally right across a field to cross two stiles in the far right-hand corner. Head down the edge of a field, passing a pond on your right. Cross another stile and then bear right to reach a gate in the far right-hand corner. Go through this and head along the right-hand side of another field to reach a road.

5 Turn left along the road, crossing a bridge over a disused railway line. At a road junction, fork right towards Over Norton. As you enter Over Norton, turn right into Quarhill Close. Follow it round as it bends left. At the far end, continue ahead between stone pillars to reach another road. Turn right, then left to reach a road junction (B4026).

6 Here, turn right along a track. Look for a sign: 'Salford 1¾'. Where the main track bends right to Cleeves Farm,

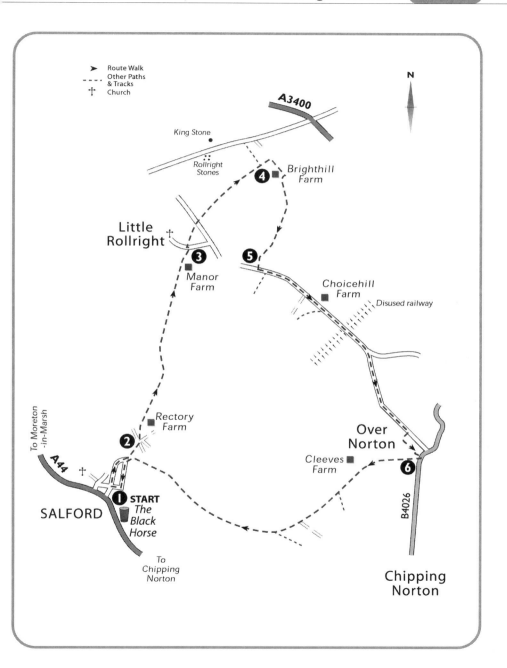

The Whispering Knights

continue ahead on a farm track running along the field edge. Ignore a track on the left and continue straight ahead. Go through a gate, the right-hand one of two, and head down the left-hand edge of two fields. About halfway down the second field the path bears left to run between hedgerows. Continue along this path, which soon widens to become a track, staying on it until you reach a road. Bear left of a small green and at a road junction, fork left downhill. The playground you passed earlier is on your right. At the bottom the road bends sharp right and soon you are back at the village hall. Pass the hall and turn left to return to the Black Horse.

Date walk completed:

....

Places of Interest

Chipping Norton, or 'Chippie' as it is known to the locals, is an interesting and picturesque market town (the word 'Chipping' means 'a market'). It is one of the gateway towns into the Cotswolds and, like its neighbour to the south, Burford, prospered as a result of the wool trade.

The **Rollright Stones**, according to one legend, resulted from witchcraft. The King, his knights and men were in the area when they came upon a witch. She informed him that if he could see the village of Long Compton from the ridge, he would become King of England. As he looked down into the valley a great mound rose before him and blocked his view. As a consequence of his failure, the King, his knights and his men were turned into stone.

Clifton (Deddington)
The Duke of Cumberland's Head

was larger than that at Banbury. The arrival of the canal and railway, which bypassed the town, was its downfall. The importance of Banbury grew, whereas that of Deddington diminished. The walk starts a few miles to the east of Deddington; at the small village of Clifton, which once had a beaver-hat factory. There are some excellent views of the undulating countryside.

Deddington was once one of Oxfordshire's most strategic and important towns. Its importance resulted in a castle being built there during the 12th century. Only the site remains today. The town had a flourishing trade in cattle, horses and sheep and its market

Distance: 5¼ miles

OS Explorer 191 Banbury, Bicester & Chipping Norton
GR 490318

A moderate walk through undulating countryside; there are a couple of gentle ascents and descents but most of the walk is on level ground

Starting point: The Duke of Cumberland's Head, Clifton. Please obtain permission if you want to use the inn car park while you walk. There is limited roadside parking in the village.

How to get there: Clifton is on the B4031 road between Deddington and Aynho. The inn is in the centre of the village.

The **Duke of Cumberland's Head** was built in the early part of the 17th century. A licensee during the 19th century ran it as a combined inn, bakery, grocery and beaver-hat shop. It is reputed that the hats proved to be so durable that nobody needed to purchase a second one and so the shop closed due to lack of business. Inside, the inn has a pleasing and comfortable atmosphere. The walls are adorned with floral prints. A separate dining area is also available. There is a large car park and beer garden at the rear. The inn provides overnight accommodation. Beers include Tetley's, Hook Norton and Adnams ales. A wide and varied selection of bar meals is available, in addition to the more substantial evening menus.

Opening times are 12 noon to 3 pm on Tuesday to Sunday and 6.30 pm to 11 pm daily (10.30 pm on Sunday). Food is available between 12 noon and 2 pm (not on a Monday) and from 7 pm to 10 pm. It is advisable to book for Sunday lunch.

Telephone: 01869 338534.

The Walk

1 With your back to the inn, cross the road and go along Chapel Close opposite. When the lane bends right, with Boulder Dyke Farm on your left, fork slightly left along a bridleway (signed 'Somerton 2¼'). The bridleway soon becomes a hedged green track. Beyond a right-hand bend, go through a gate, over a cross track, and continue along the left-hand edge of a field. If you look left, and slightly back, you should see the viaduct carrying the Banbury–Bicester railway line. At the far corner of the field, go through a gate and turn left along the field edge, turning right at the next corner. Continue ahead along the edge of a large field, over a farm track, to reach a gate in the far corner. Go through this to reach a small stream. Just to your left is Bowman's Bridge.

2 The walk at this point turns right along the edge of a field, with a hedge on your right. In 100 yards, veer left across the field to reach a gate in the opposite fence. Keep to the left of a tree on the far side. Go through the gate and continue ahead across the middle of the next field. Through another gate on the far side and then ahead along the right-hand edge of yet another field.

3 Just before reaching the far corner, turn right along a wide hedge-lined track.

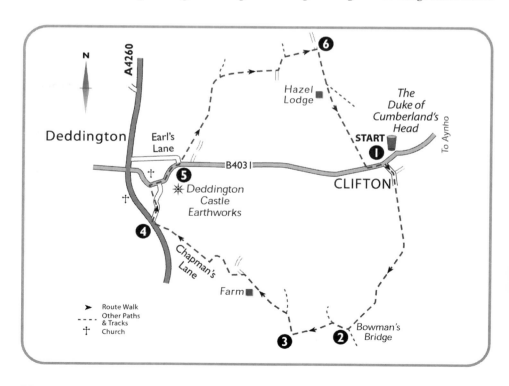

Where the hedge on the left ends, turn left along another wide track (there is a convenient tree trunk seat nearby on the right). Pass a small pond on the right and follow the track along the left-hand edge of a field towards some farm buildings. Pass to the right of the farm to join a drive. Pass to the right of some barns to reach a junction. Turn left here and in 80 yards, with the entrance to some farm buildings on the left, turn right up a farm track. The ascending track bends left and right. Stop for a rest now and again to admire the view behind you. At the top continue ahead along the track until it eventually reaches a road (A4260).

4 Turn right and, in 50 yards, bear right along St Thomas Street. On reaching a road junction continue straight ahead uphill, passing Goose Green on your left. At the T-junction, Chapel Square, bear left to reach Deddington Market Square. You now have an opportunity to investigate the town before continuing the walk. From the Market Square, return to the junction at Chapel Square. Do not turn right down Philcote Street, however, but continue ahead along the B4031, passing Featherton House (a home for retired persons), and 50 yards beyond Hopcroft Lane, on the right, a sign points the way to the site of Deddington Castle. To continue the walk, go ahead along the B4031 until you reach Earl's Lane, on the left.

5 Cross Earl's Lane, and go over the stile in the hedge on the opposite side. Cross the field, passing close to the corner of a privet hedge joining from the left. Maintain this direction across the field, passing to the left of a small clump of trees, to reach a footbridge on the far side.

Maintain direction across the next field to reach a gate and concrete farm track. Turn left along the track. Just before reaching the farm, ignore a path going off to the left, and continue ahead, passing to the right of the farm building and then between two barns to reach a farm track. Follow this farm track, along the field edge, to reach a T-junction. Here, turn left and follow the track as it bends right downhill to reach another T-junction.

6 Turn right here along Tithe Lane. Ignoring all turnings both left and right, remain on the lane until it meets the B4031 in Clifton. Turn left along the road, passing the old chapel, now used as offices, to return to the Duke of Cumberland's Head.

Places of Interest
Parts of the **church of St Peter and St Paul, Deddington** date back to the 13th century. The tower collapsed in 1635 and had to be rebuilt. Its current tower can be seen for miles around. Deddington was used as the fictional setting of the village that was razed to the ground in the television series *Blott on a Landscape*.

Only the earthworks remain of the 12th century **Deddington Castle**. During those long ago times it was the home of the de Chesney family. It was not one of our long lasting castles as it was demolished in the 14th century. Entry is free.

Date walk completed:
....

The Butchers Arms

*L*ark Rise to Candleford, written by Flora Thompson, vividly depicts Oxfordshire village life as it was in the 1880s and 1890s. This walk visits two of the villages associated with this author. Starting at Fringford, known as 'Candleford Green' in the books, the route takes you, via Hethe, to Cottisford ('Fordlow'), where Flora went to school and attended the village church. Using tracks and field paths, the walk returns to Fringford via the tiny, attractive, village of Hardwick. Flora Thompson was born at Juniper Hill ('Lark Rise') in 1876.

Distance: *6¼ miles*

OS Explorer 191 Banbury, Bicester & Chipping Norton
GR 605285

An easy walk on fairly level ground

Starting point: The Butchers Arms, Fringford.

How to get there: Fringford is north-east of Bicester. Turn north-west off the A4421 on the road signed to Fringford.

The **Butchers Arms,** overlooking the cricket pitch, is adorned with cricket paraphernalia and sports trophies. A friendly welcome greets you as you enter this typically English village inn. During the summer you can sit out at one of the bench-seat tables and watch a cricket match while you sup your Deucher's or Adnams' ale. A varied menu offers sandwiches and ciabattas, as well as steaks, chilli and other substantial fare. It can get busy at weekends especially if there is a cricket match scheduled.

Opening times during the day are 12 noon to 3 pm on Monday to Friday and Sunday and 12 noon to 5 pm on Saturday; in the evening the pub opens from 6 pm to 11 pm on Monday to Saturday and 7 pm to 10.30 pm on Sunday. Food is available from 12 noon to 2 pm and 7 pm to 9 pm daily. Only roasts are available at Sunday lunchtime and it is advisable to book for these.

Telephone: 01869 277363.

The Walk

1 With your back to the inn, go straight ahead along the road, with the cricket pitch on your right. At the road junction, bear right along The Green and in 25 yards fork left. At the road junction, on the far side of the green, go straight across and along Rectory Lane opposite. At the end of the lane, turn left through a swing gate (signed 'Hethe ¾'). Go along a short enclosed path, through a second swing gate, and bear quarter-right across a field to reach a stile and road. Turn right along the road, over Fringford Bridge.

2 Just beyond the bridge, bear left over a fenced stile (signed 'Hethe ½'). Go up the right-hand edge of a field. Cross a stile and continue ahead, now with a fence on your right. The village of Hethe can be seen directly ahead. In 150 yards, go over a stile on the right and turn left to maintain direction along the edge of the next field, with the fence now on your left. At a small sewage farm the path bends left down to a track. Turn right here and, with a small stream on your left, follow the track until you reach a road.

3 Cross the road and continue ahead across the grass opposite to reach a stile (signed 'Cottisford 1½'). Cross a stile and follow a narrow path across a wild meadow. At the far side, go over a stile in the hedge and continue ahead along the left-hand edge of a field. Ignore a gap on the left and carry straight on. Go through a gap, just to the right of the far corner, and maintain direction along the edge of the next field. There are some barns at the far side of the field, to your right. On reaching the corner of some woodland (Windmill Hook) on the left, carry straight on, keeping the wood on your left. At the next corner, go through a gap in the hedge and bear slightly left across the middle of the next field. At the far side, go over a stile and footbridge and through some bushes and scrub to another stile. After crossing this, turn right through a gate and immediately turn left. A series of stiles leads you to a gate. Go through this and bear right across a lawn, with a tennis court on your right, to reach a drive. Turn left towards the manor house and, just before the entrance, turn right to go through a gate and along another drive leading out to a road.

4 Turn left down the road, ignoring a footpath on the right, to reach Cottisford church. One of the names on the war memorial inside the church is that of Edwin Timms, younger brother of Flora Thompson, who was killed at the Battle of the Somme in 1916. Continuing on past the church you arrive at College Farm on the left.

5 Immediately after passing the farm, turn left along a farm track. Ignore all tracks leading off to the right and left and keep on the main track until you reach the corner of Tusmore Wood. At this point continue straight ahead along a bridleway running just inside the wood hedge. Go over an unsigned cross track and continue ahead to reach a signed cross track.

6 Here, turn left through a gap in the hedge and follow a path across the field towards Hardwick. Where the path divides, take the right-hand fork and continue ahead. Pass through a small paddock and out to a road. Cross the road and go along the track opposite

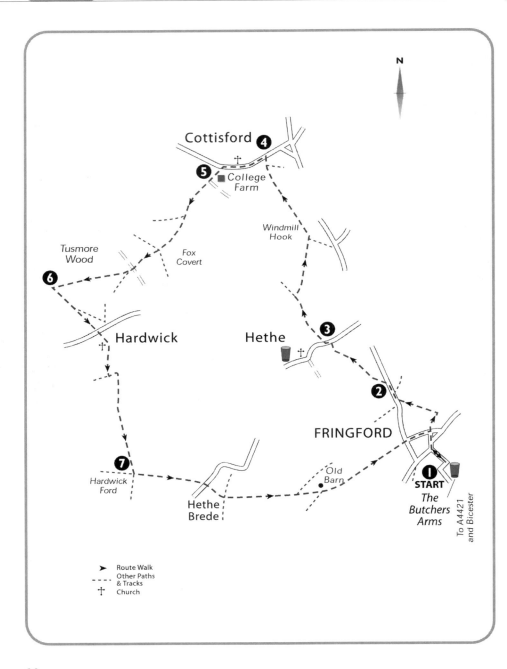

N

Cottisford ❹

❺ ☩
College
Farm

Windmill
Hook

Tusmore
Wood

Fox
Covert

❻

Hardwick ☩

Hethe ☩

❸

❷

FRINGFORD

❼

Hardwick
Ford

Old
Barn

❶
START
*The
Butchers
Arms*

To A4421
and Bicester

Hethe
Brede

➤   Route Walk
- - -   Other Paths
     & Tracks
☩   Church

Cottisford church where Flora Thompson once worshipped

(signed 'Stoke Lyne 1¼'). Pass Hardwick church and, at a work-yard, turn right along a track, soon with open fields on your left and a ditch and hedge on your right. At the far end of the field bear right past a post with a bridleway sign to reach a cross track just inside a small copse. Turn left and in 50 yards, at the next junction, turn right to reach an open field. Continue along the left-hand edge of two fields to reach a gate and footbridge (Hardwick Ford).

7 On the far side, ignore a track going right and continue ahead for 20 yards before turning left. The path now follows the left edge of a few large fields before reaching a road at Hethe Brede. Cross the road and go along the track opposite, passing between barns to reach a gate. Go through and bear slightly left across two fields, soon with a stream on your left. Where the stream bends left, go through a gate and ahead across another field, heading towards the ruins of an old barn, ignoring a path veering off to the left. Pass to the right of the barn and keep ahead along a farm track. Stay on this track until you reach a road. Cross this and walk along the road opposite. At Fringford's green, turn right along the right-hand edge to reach a road junction. Cross to the pavement opposite and follow it back to the Butchers Arms.

Place of Interest

Bicester is a busy market town with a long history. To the south-west of the town is Bicester Village, a factory designer outlet shopping centre.

Date walk completed:

. . . .

The Bell Inn

and the Oxford Canal presents a pleasant start to the walk before heading to the hilltop village of Steeple Aston, passing the Rousham Eyecatcher folly en-route. From Steeple Aston the route heads south and passes close to Rousham House and Park before returning to Lower Heyford.

The **Bell Inn**, which dates from the early 17th century, was once a chapel. The main bar has three separate areas where customers can dine and drink in comfort. A dresser displays a handsome collection of hand-bells. There is also a games room and a small garden at the rear. Beers include Bass, Adnams Broadside and Abbot Ale from Greene King. A varied selection of food is available

This delightful walk in the Cherwell Valley starts at the village of Lower Heyford. Its name is thought to derive from the fact that it was once an important river crossing place for farmers after gathering in their hay. A stretch between the river

Opening times are 11.30 am to 3 pm and 6 pm to 11 pm on Monday to Saturday; 12 noon to 3 pm and 7 pm to 10.30 pm on Sunday. The availability of food tends to keep fairly close to the pub opening hours. The pub is very popular with canal users and it is advisable to book on a weekend.

Telephone: 01869 347176.

Distance: *5 miles*

OS Explorer 191 Banbury, Bicester & Chipping Norton
GR 486248

This is a relatively easy walk with a few short ascents and descents

Starting point: The Bell Inn. Park near the pub, or in Church Lane.

How to get there: Lower Heyford is situated on the B4030, west of Bicester. Turn off just east of the Oxford Canal to reach the Market Square and the Bell.

The Walk

1 With your back to the Bell, turn left and almost immediately turn left again into Freehold Street, with its picturesque ironstone cottages. In 300 yards, branch left down Mill Lane to reach a drawbridge over the Oxford Canal. Cross the bridge and turn right along the canal towpath. In 200 yards the River Cherwell appears on your left. For the next mile the path runs between the river, on the left, and the canal, on the right. After about ½ mile a church tower and an old tithe barn, at Upper Heyford, come into view over to your right. Walking 200 yards beyond Allen's Lock, you reach a bridge, numbered 203.

2 Turn left here, leaving the canal, to cross a bridge over the River Cherwell.

Veer right across the field to reach a second bridge over another arm of the river. Cross this and immediately turn right, keeping the river on your right. Pass under the Oxford to Banbury railway line and then head across a field, aiming towards some woodland. The Cherwell, which makes a large loop at this point, rejoins us before we reach the woodland.

3 When you are about 40 yards short of the woodland, turn left to reach, and cross, a stile and footbridge. Go through a small belt of trees and up a bank to reach a field. Head up the field, aiming towards the left-hand side of a line of trees at the top. Go through a gap in the hedge and immediately turn right along the field edge. Over to your left is the buttressed three-arched folly known as the Rousham Eyecatcher. Built by William Kent, as a

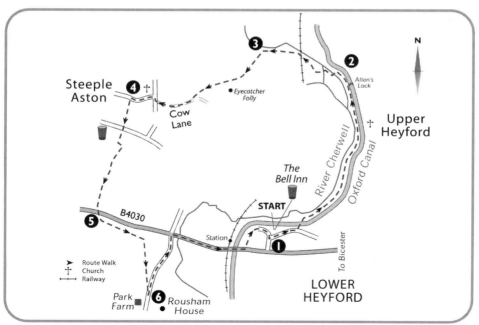

focus for the view along the Cherwell Valley from Rousham House, just over a mile away, it certainly lives up to its name. With trees on your right, follow the field edge down and around to reach a gate. After passing through, turn right along Cow Lane to reach a road junction, with Steeple Aston church diagonally opposite to your right. Cross the road, diagonally right, and go along Northside, passing to the left of the church.

4 In 300 yards, just after passing a post box in the wall on the right, turn left down a narrow enclosed path. At the bottom go through a swing gate, over a small stream, then up a field to a gate in the top left-hand corner. Go along another enclosed path, between houses to reach a road. (*Turn right if you wish to visit the Red Lion pub.*) Cross the road diagonally left to the path opposite (signed 'Rousham 1¼'). Go over a stone stile, up a bank then swing left to reach a metalled drive. Now turn right. Where the drive turns left, continue straight ahead. Pass a barn on your left, keeping to the left of a telegraph post. Maintain direction across a field, passing just to the right of a fenced well. Go through a gap on the far side and steeply down through bushes to reach a stile and field. Keep to the left-hand side of the field to reach a stile in the top left-hand corner, with a road just beyond.

5 Cross the road and up the bank on the opposite side. At the top, turn left along a wooded path to reach a stile on the right. Go over and bear diagonally left across the field, keeping to the left of a group of lime trees, then a small plantation, to reach the far left-hand corner of the field, near Park Farm. Go out onto the road.

6 Turn left along the road, keeping the boundary wall of Rousham Park on your right. At a crossroads, turn right along the B4030, crossing Heyford Bridge over the River Cherwell. Continuing ahead you soon get a good view of Rousham House over to your right. Shortly after passing over the railway and the Oxford Canal, turn left through a swing gate and along the left-hand side of a field. Where the wall on the left ends, continue straight ahead to reach a corner of a garden coming in from the right. Keeping the gardens on your right, follow the fence round when it bends right to reach a swing gate. Go through this and along a short enclosed path. Go through another swing gate, turn left and almost immediately turn right. Follow Church Lane, past the church, to return to the Bell Inn, which will be on your left.

Place of Interest
Rousham Park House and Garden: Sir Robert Dormer built the house in 1635. William Kent (1685–1748) added the wings and stable block. It is, however, Kent's landscape garden that is the highlight of this property. It represents one of the earliest phases of English landscape design and has been kept very much as he left it. The house is open between April and September on Wednesdays, Sundays and Bank Holiday Mondays between 2 pm and 4.30 pm. The garden is open daily between 10 am and 4.30 pm throughout the year. Telephone: 01869 347110 or 01993 813276 (tourist information).

Date walk completed:

....

Shipton-under-Wychwood 27 Walk

The Shaven Crown Hotel

Jacobean manor house, is a picturesque village in the Oxfordshire Cotswolds. Leaving Shipton the walk visits Milton-Under-Wychwood before heading north-east, where it meets up with the Oxfordshire Way, which is then followed back to Shipton, passing Bruern Abbey. Built in 1720, this is now a private school.

The **Shaven Crown Hotel** near the start of the walk,

The ancient forest of Wychwood was once one of the four largest tracts of woodland in the country. Today very little of this forest exists, much of the land being cleared for agricultural use. New plantations are currently being laid to try to reinstate some of the lost woodland. Shipton-Under-Wychwood, with its large

is a traditional English village inn built of local honey-coloured Cotswold stone. It was originally built about 1300 as a hostelry for the monks of the nearby monastery at Bruern. Following the dissolution of the monastery by Henry VIII in 1534, Elizabeth I used the building as a hunting lodge. She presented it to the village in 1580 when it became an inn. Beers include Greene King, Hook Norton and Fuller's ale. The Shaven Crown serves an imaginative array of bar food and children are welcome.

Opening times are 11.30 am to 2.30 pm and 5 pm to 11 pm every day. Bar meals are served between 12 noon and 2 pm and 5.30 pm to 9.30 pm. The restaurant is open for lunch on Sunday between 12 noon and 2 pm and every day for dinner from 7 pm to 9 pm.

Telephone: 01993 832136.

Distance: *6¾ miles*

*OS Explorer OL 45 The Cotswolds
GR 279179*

This is a moderate walk through gently undulating countryside

Starting point: Church Street, near the church of St Mary the Virgin, in Shipton.

How to get there: Shipton-under-Wychwood is situated on the A361 north of Burford. Church Street leads off to the right of the green, in the village. Roadside parking is available.

The Walk

1 With the green on your right, go along Church Lane to the A361. Note the Victorian drinking fountain on the green, with the Shaven Crown Hotel directly opposite. The fountain was erected 'in memory of 17 parishioners who perished when their ship, *Cospatric,* caught fire on its journey to New Zealand'. Turn left along the A361 and follow it gently uphill for ¼ mile. Pass Shipton Court (manor house) on the left and follow the road round a sharp right-hand bend. When the road bends left, continue straight ahead along a broad path, signposted to Milton-under-Wychwood. Pass a gate on the left leading into Diggers Wood, a site purchased by the Woodland Trust in 2000 as part of the restoration of Wychwood Forest. Once the hedged path opens out there are some good views over the woods and fields of the Evenlode Valley. At the top of a short rise the path veers half-right. Go through a swing gate and bear left between wire fences down to a small stream. Cross a footbridge and stile, then bear half-right across two fields towards Milton-under-Wychwood. On reaching a road, continue straight ahead along Jubilee Lane, passing The Sands on the right, to reach a T-junction.

2 Turn right. In 30 yards, turn left between houses (signed 'Fifield 1½'). The path crosses three fields, following a line of telegraph posts. Go through a gate and continue ahead along a farm track until you reach a road, at Grange Farm.

3 Turn right here and follow a pleasant country road, passing Home Farm on your left, until you reach a junction. Now swing left in the direction of Bruern for 100 yards, to reach a bridleway on the left, signed 'Bould 1' and 'D'Arcy Dalton Way'.

4 Turn left through a gate and head straight across the field. Go through a gap in the hedge on the far side, then bear slightly left across the next field keeping just to the left of a small copse of Scots pines. At the far side, the path passes through a small belt of trees and emerges at the edge of another field. Turn right and follow the path round two sides of the field. In the far right corner, turn left and in 15 yards turn right to enter Foxholes Nature Reserve. Continue ahead for 200 yards to reach a multi-path junction. There is a tree trunk seat and a wooden barrier on your left. Our route turns right, however, following the direction of a blue arrow. Pass a path going off left and continue ahead to reach a junction. Here, ignore the direction indicated by a blue arrow and fork right along the edge of the wood. Follow the path, then a drive, to reach a cross track, with a small car park just opposite. Turn left, and in 5 yards, turn right along the edge of the car park into more trees to reach a cross path.

5 Here, we turn right to follow the Oxfordshire Way back to Shipton-under-Wychwood. At first the path meanders through trees, then along the edge of a field to reach a road. Cross the road and go through the gate opposite into parkland. Bruern Abbey can be seen to your left. Bear quarter-left to pass between the boundary fence of the abbey and a small fenced enclosure. Continue ahead to pass through a gate and across the middle of a field towards some woodland. Go through a gap and head

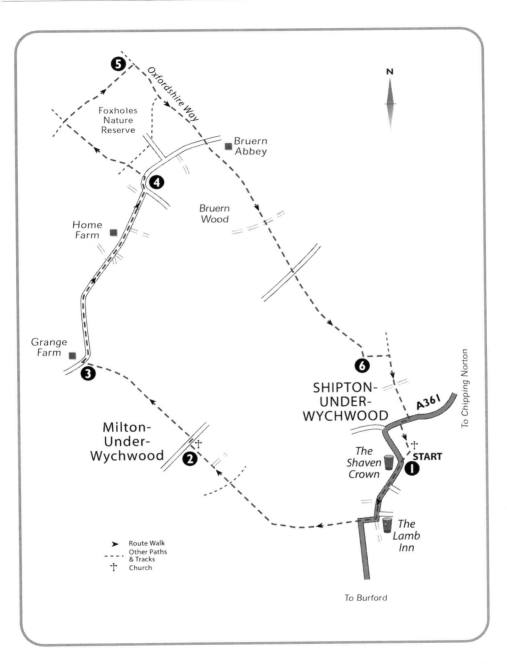

N

❺

Oxfordshire Way

Foxholes
Nature
Reserve

■ Bruern
Abbey

❹

Bruern
Wood

Home
Farm ■

Grange
Farm ■

❸

Milton-
Under-
Wychwood

† ❷

❻

SHIPTON-
UNDER-
WYCHWOOD

A361

To Chipping Norton

The
Shaven
Crown

† **START**

❶

The
Lamb
Inn

To Burford

➤ Route Walk
---- Other Paths
      & Tracks
† Church

Bruern Abbey

along a wide ride through Bruern Wood. Look behind you for an excellent view of Bruern Abbey. At the far end of the ride, go through a gate in the left-hand corner and through some bushes. A clear path leads you across two fields, over a lane, and then across three more fields to reach a hedge corner.

6 Turn left, keeping the hedge on your right, to reach a farm track. Turn right and follow the track until, just after crossing a stream, it merges with a road

in Shipton. Continue along the road to its junction with the A361, where you turn right. In 80 yards turn left along Church Path. (*If you wish to visit the Red Horse pub continue along the A361.*) Pass the church and turn right along Church Street to return to the village green.

Date walk completed:

....

Places of Interest

Burford, gateway to the Cotswolds, is situated just to the south of Shipton-under-Wychwood. The **Tolsey Museum**, in the High Street, has a wide collection of artefacts and exhibits illustrating the town's social and industrial past. It is open between April and October. Tuesday–Friday and Sundays: 2 pm to 5 pm; Saturdays: 11 am to 5 pm. Telephone: 01993 823196.

Minster Lovell Hall ruins are situated between Burford and Witney. It is reputed that King Richard III and Henry VII both stayed at this once fine manor house. The ruins, and a nearby dovecot, are both in the care of English Heritage and can be visited at any time.

of visitors. Although this walk does not take in this fine stately home it does have the attraction of passing close to the ruins of an old Roman villa, at North Leigh. From there, the route heads north towards Stonesfield, a village associated with slate quarrying. Joining the Oxfordshire Way, the walk follows this long distance path to Blenheim Great Park where we leave it to return to Combe.

Combe, an unspoilt village on the eastern fringe of the Cotswolds, has retained most of its rural character. Situated close to Blenheim Palace and Park it attracts a fair number

The **Cock Inn** is a traditional Cotswold pub and its two bars have a pleasant, friendly ambience. Beers include Greene King IPA, Ruddles County and Suffolk Summer (a seasonal ale). You can enjoy these inside or, on fine days, on the bench seats outside or, if there is room, on a seat around the trunk of a tree on the green. A good choice of food is on offer to whet your appetite. Booking is essential for Sunday lunches.

Distance: 5½ miles

OS Explorer 180 Oxford, Witney & Woodstock
GR 412159

This is a relatively easy walk in gently rolling countryside

Starting point: The Cock Inn. Please obtain permission if you want to use the pub car park while you walk. There is some limited parking near the inn.

How to get there: Combe is situated off the A4095 between Witney and the A44 south of Woodstock. Leave the A4095 at Long Hanborough and follow the signs, north, to Combe. The inn overlooks the large village green.

Opening times are 12 noon to 3 pm and 6 pm to 11 pm on Monday to Friday; 11.30 am to 4 pm and 6 pm to 11 pm on Saturday; all day on Sunday. Lunchtime food is available from 12 noon to 2.30 pm on Monday to Friday; 12 noon to 4 pm on Saturday; 12 noon to 3 pm on Sunday. In the evenings (Tuesday to Saturday only) it is served from 6 pm until 8.45 pm.

Telephone: 01993 891288.

The Walk

1 With your back to the inn, turn right. Pass the village hall and veer right on a tarmac path across a small green. At the road, turn right and in 30 yards, at a junction, fork right and keep ahead. Look out for a notice on the left stating 'Site of the Village Pound'. Pass Chatterspie Lane, on the right, and continue ahead, passing a footpath sign indicating 'North Leigh – East End 1½'. After passing between a farmhouse and a barn, the track descends fairly steeply. Remain on the track until you reach Lower Westfield Farm.

2 Just beyond the farmhouse, where the track bends right, continue straight ahead through a gate. Follow a farm track along the edge of a field, bending right and descending to reach the River Evenlode. At the bottom, with the river on your left, go ahead for about 30 yards to reach a bridge over the river. Cross this and immediately turn left along the field edge to reach and go over a stile in the field corner. Go under the railway, over another stile and then bear half-right across a field, leaving the river. Cross a stile and footbridge on the far side and continue up the edge of the next field.

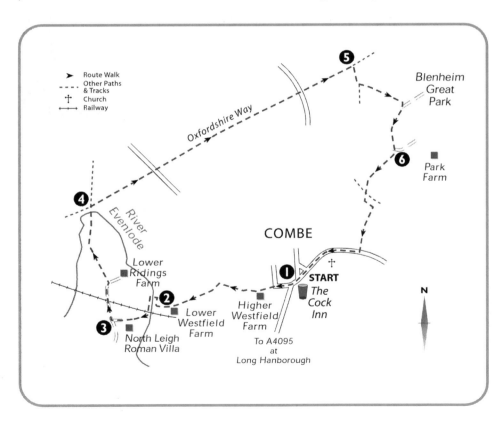

North Leigh Roman Villa

Through the hedge on your left you will soon see parts of the North Leigh Roman Villa. In 100 yards, turn left over a stile. (*The entrance to the site of the villa is a few yards ahead on your left.*) Turn right up to a track T-junction.

3 Turn right along the track, passing over the railway this time. Where the track bends right to Lower Ridings Farm, continue straight ahead, through a gate and along the edge of a field. On the hillside ahead you can see the village of Stonesfield. Where the hedge on the right ends, continue straight ahead to reach a gate. Go through the gate and bear half-right across the field to reach a bridge over the River Evenlode. Cross the bridge

and head up the edge of the field on the far side. In 30 yards, look for a swing gate on the right. (*If you wish to visit Stonesfield to see its 13th century church and Cotswold stone houses or simply for some liquid refreshment, continue straight on up the field. This will add about a mile to the walk.*)

4 Turn right through the gate. You have now joined the Oxfordshire Way. The path contours round the foot of a bank to reach another swing gate. Go through this and along the edge of a field. A clear path follows the edge of another two fields to reach a road. Cross the road and maintain direction along the left-hand edge of a large field, then between fields to reach another road. Go straight across and along the right-hand edge of the field opposite to reach a ladder stile. Go over this into Blenheim Great Park.

5 In 20 yards, at a cross track, turn right, leaving the Oxfordshire Way. The track runs through a strip of woodland. In 150 yards, turn left to go over a flat wooden bridge. On emerging at the edge of a field, turn right along the field edge. Where the trees on your right end, continue straight ahead between fields towards some woodland. On reaching the wood edge, turn right and follow a track round the edge of the wood to reach a track T-junction.

6 Turn right here, following the track across a field, passing just to the left of a telegraph pole. At the far side, bear left along the field edge. At the field corner, continue straight ahead into woodland.

The path drops down to reach a cross track. Bear left over this track and follow a faint path on the other side to join a wider track, now ascending more steeply uphill. Where a track joins from the right, bear left for 15 yards to reach a marker post on the right. Bear right here to go over another ladder stile. Turn left along the field edge, with the boundary wall on your left. In 40 yards, turn right up the right-hand edge of a field to reach a road. Turn right along the road, passing a Methodist church and a playground on the left. The road bends left and right before you eventually return to the village green, and the Cock Inn.

Date walk completed:

....

Place of Interest

Blenheim Palace, Park and Garden, Woodstock: Built in 1704 for John Churchill, the 1st Duke of Marlborough, from a design by Sir John Vanbrugh, the palace is one of the largest and finest works of Baroque architecture in the country. Capability Brown landscaped the park and created the lake in 1764. Sir Winston Churchill, who is buried at the church of St Martin in the nearby village of Bladon, was born at Blenheim Palace. The palace and gardens are open between mid-March and October. Telephone: 01993 811091.

The Star Inn

village, has some interesting carved bench ends of human heads and grotesque animals. Across the road from the church is Rectory Farm House where John White, the founder of the colony of Massachusetts, New England, was born in 1575. This countryside walk heads south to the village of Holton. The return route passes through Forest Hill, or Forstel as it was recorded in the Domesday Book.

It is hard to believe that the thriving village of Stanton St John and the surrounding countryside is situated just five miles north-east of Oxford. The church of St John the Baptist, in the

Distance: 5½ miles

OS Explorer 180 Oxford, Witney & Woodstock
GR 578090

A fairly level walk, mainly across fields and farmland

Starting point: The Star Inn. Please obtain permission if you want to use the pub car park while you walk. Parking is also available in the village hall car park, near the church.

How to get there: Stanton St John is situated 5 miles north-east of Oxford, just off the B4027 Wheatley to Islip road. The Star Inn is on the left, in Middle Road, as you enter the village from the south.

The **Star Inn** is a traditional 17th century village inn, with flagstone floors, dark oak furniture and log fires burning during the winter months. Half a dozen steps lead down to a second bar and two separate dining areas, one a conservatory. The inn has a well-maintained beer garden, with a children's play area. Extensive lunch and evening menus, including vegetarian options, are available. Being a Wadworth's pub, the ales include 6X, Henry's Smooth and Henry's IPA.

Opening times are 11 pm to 2.30 pm and 6.30 pm to 11 pm on Monday to Saturday; 12 noon to 2.30 pm and 7 pm to 10.30 pm on Sunday. Food is available from 12 noon to 2 pm and 7 pm to 9.30 pm every day.

Telephone: 01865 351277.

The Walk

1 Leave the inn car park and turn left downhill, following the road round as it bends left. Pass the Village Stores on the left and continue ahead to reach the village hall car park on the right. (*Rectory Farmhouse is on the right-hand corner of the road junction just beyond. A plaque over the front door reads: 'The birthplace of John White, 1575–1648, Fellow of New College, Oxford, and chief founder of the colony of Massachusetts, New England'.*) Turn right through the car park and go through the gate at the far side. Bear slightly left down the field to reach a footbridge just to the left of a telegraph pole. Bear slightly left across the next field, following the line of overhead telegraph wires, to reach another footbridge and stile, just to the right of a field corner. Continue along the edge of the next field, still using the telegraph wires as a guide. In 300 yards, turn left over a stile, beside a gate, onto a road. Turn right along the road for 600 yards.

2 At a footpath sign (Holton 2½) turn right through a gate and head across the field to the far right-hand corner. Go through a wide gap and continue along the edge of Stanton Great Wood until you reach its very far corner.

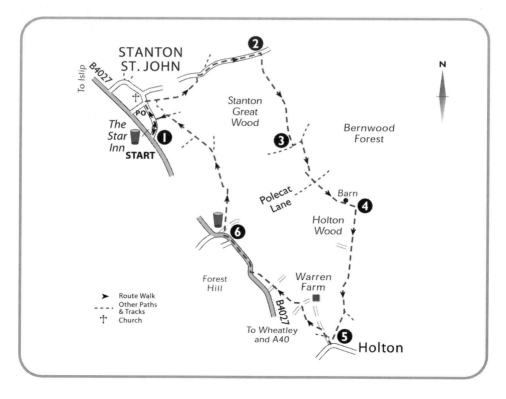

Rectory Farmhouse, the birthplace of John White

3 Here, cross an earth bridge and immediately turn left along the field edge, with a ditch on your left. At the field corner turn right, still keeping the ditch on your left. At the next field corner, turn right past a willow tree and in 20 yards turn left through a gap, over another ditch. Now bear left to rejoin the main ditch and continue ahead along the field edge. At the far side, go through a gate and over an old wooden bridge to reach a cross track (Polecat Lane). Go straight across and over the stile opposite. Walk along the right-hand edge of the next field to reach a corner of Holton Wood. Here, bear left along a farm track, heading towards a barn, with the wood on your right. Pass to the right of the barn and in 100 yards look for a gate on the right.

4 Turn right through the gate and follow a wide firebreak up through Holton Wood. At the far side of the wood continue ahead across the middle of a large field. Bear slightly right across a second, smaller, field to go through a gap and over a small stream at the far side. Go over a stile and head across the next field towards a hedge corner. Go through a gap in the hedge and trees and continue along the right-hand edge of the next field. At the far side, go through another gap and, ignoring a path veering off to the left, continue ahead across the next field towards a hedge corner. Maintain direction across the field, passing under some telegraph wires. At the far side follow the path through some trees and scrub to reach a road.

5 Turn right and, almost immediately, turn right again along a track leading to Warren Farm. Ignore a path going off left and continue ahead over a cattle grid and along the farm drive. At a 'Private Road' sign, veer left across the field and then turn right along the field edge. When parallel with the farm, go over a stile and bear slightly right across the field and a farm track to reach a stile at the edge of a copse. Follow a path through the copse and then along the edge of a field. A short enclosed section leads to a track, with a cottage just to your left. Cross the track and go through the gate opposite. Continue ahead and, where the copse on your right ends, veer left across the field to the left-hand hedge. Now turn right. Just 20 yards before reaching the field corner, turn left over a stile to a road. Turn right to enter Forest Hill.

6 Just before the White Horse Inn, fork right to Minchin Court, then turn right down a track. In 80 yards, turn left up some steps and bear slightly right across a field. Go through a gap on the far side and maintain direction across the next field. At the far side go down a few steps, over a footbridge, then bear left of a derelict farm building to the left-hand hedge. Now turn right, with the hedge on your left, and follow a track along the edge of three fields aiming towards the radio mast at Beckley. At the far side of the third field, turn left to join a road and at the road junction, turn left uphill to return to the Star Inn.

> **Place of Interest**
> Oxford, 'city of dreaming spires', has so much to offer that one can spend days looking around its various attractions. Amongst its many museums are the Ashmolean, the Bate Collection of Musical Instruments and the University Botanic Garden. There are the fascinating buildings of the various University Colleges and numerous churches. Or perhaps you may prefer to relax beside the tranquil River Thames.

Date walk completed:

....

The Plough Inn

Kencot. The latter has won 'Best Kept Village' awards on a number of occasions. The return to Alvescot takes you through more agricultural fields. The terrain is quite level so you will not get any great views but each village has an attraction that draws you to it.

The village of Alvescot is situated just to the south-west of Brize Norton airfield, so you may have an opportunity of spotting a few aircraft during this walk. Field paths and quiet country lanes take you to the local stone villages of Langford, Broadwell and

Distance: *5¾ miles*

OS Explorer OL45 The Cotswolds
GR 271046

This is an easy walk over fairly level countryside

Starting point: The Plough Inn. Please obtain permission if you want to use the pub car park while you walk. Some roadside parking is available in the village.

How to get there: Take the A4095 between Bampton and Faringdon. At Clanfield, turn north along the B4020 to Alvescot. The inn is on the right in the centre of the village.

The **Plough** is a partly 17th century village pub with a wonderful floral display in summer. The carpeted bar has a large antique case of stuffed birds of prey and a display of china ornaments, and a number of aircraft photographs adorn the walls. A two part dining area provides ample room for eating in comfort. At the rear of the inn there is a small dovecot and a little garden with a children's slide. A varied menu, which includes vegetarian and children's meals, is on offer. Beer includes Wadworth 6X and IPA. The landlord holds the key for the church, which is directly opposite the pub.

Opening times at lunchtime are 11.30 am to 3 pm on Monday to Friday; 11 am to 3 pm on Saturday; 12 noon to 3 pm on Sunday. In the evening the pub opens from 6 pm to 11 pm on Monday to Saturday and 7 pm to 10.30 pm on Sunday. Food is available from 12 noon to 2 pm every day and from 6.30 pm to 9 pm on Monday to Saturday; 7 pm to 8.30 pm on Sunday.

Telephone: 01993 842281.

The Walk

1 With your back to the inn, turn left along the road. Just after passing Red Lion House, turn right across the road and along a minor road just opposite, signed to Lower End. At a junction, fork right, passing a footpath on the left. After a sharp bend, at Walnut Cottage, continue straight ahead along a bridleway, which soon becomes a hedge-lined track. Ignore a gate directly ahead and remain on the track as it forks left. Where the track emerges into an open field, bear slightly right to join a path running between a narrow band of trees. At the far end, go through a gate and along the edge of a field. Bazeland Farm can be seen ahead to your left. Continue

ahead along the edge of the next field to reach Calcroft Lane.

2 Turn right along the lane, passing the drive to Edgerly Farm on the left. Shortly you cross a bridge that took the lane over a now dismantled railway line. Ignoring paths going off to the right and left, continue round a sharp right-hand bend, passing the buildings of Broadwell Mill Farm on the left. Where the lane takes another sharp turn to the right, turn left at a footpath sign. Go over a stile and, taking the left-hand path, head across the field towards the far left-hand corner. Here, cross a footbridge on the left taking you over Broadwell Brook. Continue ahead along the left-hand side of two fields to reach a stile. Cross this and carry

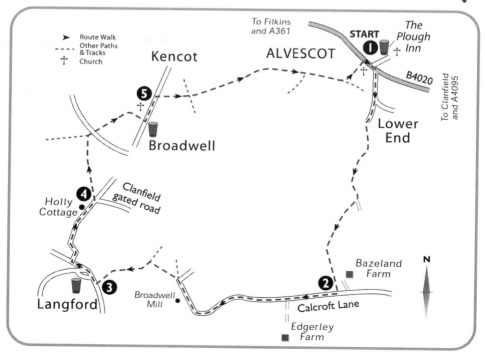

on along a track, with a wall on the right, to reach a road. You have now arrived at Langford.

3 Turn right along the road, passing the Bell Inn and a road on the left. At the next road junction – note the stone cross on the green – continue straight ahead towards Filkins. At the next junction, turn right towards Broadwell. Where the road bends sharp left, go over a stile and head straight across the field. Cross over a footbridge, with a stile at each end, and bear left across the next field, aiming to the left of a thatched cottage. Cross a stile in the field corner and out onto a road. Turn right along the road, passing Holly Cottage, to reach Clanfield Gated Road on the right.

4 Just beyond this road, turn left over a footbridge and stile and then bear diagonally right across a field towards the right-hand corner of a wood. Cross a stile in the field corner and turn left through a gated gap. Now bear diagonally right across the field to reach a road. Cross the road and over the stone stile opposite. Note the D'Arcy Dalton Way sign. Walk along the edge of the field, aiming just to the left of Broadwell church. Cross a stile in the right-hand fence and head across the grass to a drive. Turn right and follow the drive out to a road. The Five Bells pub is just over to your right. Turn left along the road through Broadwell and into Kencot where, 80 yards beyond the village sign, you should look for a footpath sign (Alvescot 1¼) on the right.

5 Turn right here. Pass between a house and garden and walk along the right-hand edge of a playground. Go through a gate and head across the field towards a fence

corner. Go over a stile and maintain your direction on an enclosed path, which runs between a fence and a wall. Where the fence bends left continue ahead. Go over a stone stile and bear slightly left across a field to a stone stile in the far corner. Cross a farm track and head along the edge of the next field towards Alvescot. Maintaining direction the path now crosses three fields, with stiles in between each one. At the far side of the third field, go over a stile, through a gap in the hedge and then bear left across a small field. Go over a stile in the fence and continue ahead, with a sports field on your right. Go over a stile on the right, passing a hall on your left, to reach a gate and road. Turn left to return to the Plough Inn.

Place of Interest

Swinford Museum, Filkins has a fine collection of local agricultural, domestic and trade and craft tools. It is open from May to September between 2.30 pm and 5 pm or by arrangement. Admission is free. Telephone: 01367 860209.

Cotswold Wildlife Park, situated just off the A361 south of Burford, has a wide range of animals, insects, reptiles and mammals. The park is open from 10 am every day except Christmas Day, until 4.30 pm in March to September or until 3 pm in October to February. There is an admission charge but car parking is free. Telephone: 01993 823006.

Date walk completed:

. . . .

The Bat and Ball Inn

This walk, taking in two of South Oxfordshire's picturesque hilltop villages, provides a succession of extensive views of the Thames Valley to the south and west of Cuddesdon, where the walk starts. From Cuddesdon, well known for its theological college built by George Street in 1854, the route takes you, via Denton, to the medieval village of Garsington, which had connections with the literary group known as the 'Bloomsbury Set'. You will be walking in the footsteps of many well-known writers, including D.H. Lawrence and Virginia Woolf, who were visitors here.

Distance: *4 miles*

OS Explorer 180 Oxford, Witney & Woodstock
GR 598029

A moderate walk through gently undulating countryside

Starting point: The Bat and Ball Inn. Please obtain permission if you want to use the inn car park while you walk. Some roadside parking is also available nearby.

How to get there: From the A40(T) east of Oxford, take the road south through Wheatley, signed to Garsington, and in approximately 1 mile turn left to Cuddesdon. On entering the village take a right fork; the inn will be on the left.

The **Bat and Ball Inn** is an old coaching inn. It has a cosy and smart interior boasting a large selection of cricket memorabilia, which adorn the walls and ceilings. It is a haven, and a delight, for the cricket enthusiast. With pine tables and flagstone floors the bar has a comfortable feel. The inn provides B&B accommodation and all the rooms are named after well-known cricketers. Children and dogs are welcome. Beers include Marston's Pedigree and other hand-pulled ales. A good selection of food is displayed on menu boards.

Opening times are 11 am until 11 pm (10.30 pm on Sunday). Food is served from 11.30 am to 2.30 pm and 6.30 pm to 9.30 pm.

Telephone: 01865 874379.

The Walk

1 Facing the Bat and Ball Inn, turn right along the road. In 50 yards, turn left into a playing field (signed 'Chippinghurst 1'). Bear half-right across the field, passing to the left of a children's play area. At the far side, go down a bank, through some bushes and trees, and over a small footbridge. Head along the right-hand edge of a field and, where the hedge on the right bends right, continue straight on across the field. In 250 yards, approximately halfway across the field, turn right at a faint cross path. Aim just to the right of some distant farm buildings. Go over a footbridge and two stiles to reach a road. Turn left and at a road junction,

with Lower Farm just opposite, turn left again.

2 Where the buildings of Lower Farm end, turn right to go over a stile beside a farm gate. Pass between some barns and continue ahead along a track, gradually ascending. At a track junction, turn right and, in 30 yards, at the field corner, turn left along the field edge. At the far corner, turn left, and in 30 yards, turn right through a gap in the hedge. Go straight across the field, aiming towards the left edge of a row of trees. At the far side, you should find yourself at a small corner of the field. Go through a gap in the hedge on your left then bear quarter-right across the next field. Aim just to the left of a telegraph pole. On reaching a hedge corner, follow

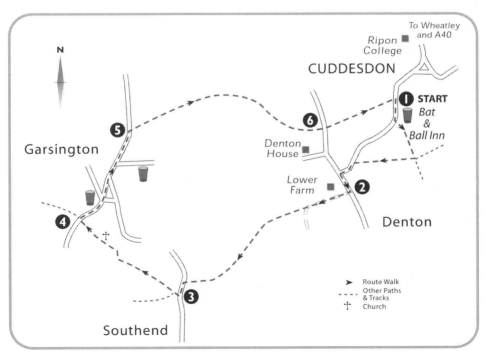

the field edge, keeping the hedge on your right. Cross a stone stile in the corner and continue along an enclosed path, then a drive, to reach a road. Turn left for 150 yards towards Southend village.

3 Just past a small post box, turn right over a stile and bear half-right up the field, passing just to the left of a small ringed enclosure. At the far corner, go through a gate on the left and along a wide enclosed stretch to reach a stile on the right, at the far end. Cross the stile and follow the path through some bushes and trees, over a small stream, and then up some steps to emerge at the edge of a field. Garsington church is directly ahead of you. Head up the field towards the church but veer left just before reaching it. There is an excellent view from this vantage point. With the church on your right, head towards a thatched cottage. Pass to the right of the garden wall, through a swing gate and along an enclosed path to a road.

4 Turn right up the road, with care. Pass the Plough pub on the left, and at the road junction continue straight ahead uphill towards the war memorial. When you reach the war memorial, take a short detour along the road to your right, called The Green. Here you will see, on the right, a medieval cross thought to date back to around 1240. Opposite the cross are the Three Horseshoes pub and a covered display board relating the history of Garsington, together with a map. Return to The Hill and turn right. Pass Denton Lane and North Manor Estate on the right and in 150 yards look for a footpath sign (to Denton) on the right.

5 Turn right down a track, through a garage area and over a stile. Go across a small field, over another stile, and along the right-hand edge of a field. There is a good view of Ripon Ecclesiastic College up on the hill in Cuddesdon from here. In 100 yards, go over a stile on the right and immediately turn left along the field edge, with a hedge now on your left. Cross a stile in the corner and bear slightly right across the next field. Cross two stiles and a footbridge, then bear half-right across the next field, keeping to the left of a telegraph pole. Maintain direction across the next two fields to a reach a stile in the corner. Now go along an enclosed path, passing a house on the left, to reach a lane.

6 Turn right, and in 10 yards, bear left along a narrow path. In 5 yards, turn left over a stone bridge and stile and head up the field, keeping well to the left of some barns. Go over a stile, to the right of a gate, and along the edge of a field. Cross a stile at the far side and walk ahead between houses to reach a road. Turn left uphill to return to the Bat and Ball Inn.

Place of Interest

Waterperry Gardens, situated just north of Wheatley, is within easy reach via the M40. The gardens are open from 9 am all year, to 5.30 pm in March to October and to 5 pm in November to February. In addition to the gardens there is an art gallery and a small museum with a fine collection of agricultural tools - also a garden shop and a teashop. Telephone: 01844 339226.

Date walk completed:

....

The Crown Inn

Book. This fascinating walk takes you across fields and meadows, and along a disused railway to the outskirts of the delightful market town of Thame. A short diversion from the route presents you with an opportunity to investigate some of the interesting architecture to be found there. The walk returns to Sydenham via Thame Park and New Park.

A large part of the village of Sydenham is designated a conservation area due to its many listed buildings. A plaque on the wall of the Old School Room states that the community is recorded in the Domesday

Distance: *6¼ miles*

OS Explorer 181 Chiltern Hills North and 180 Oxford, Witney & Woodstock
GR 730018

This is an easy walk on fairly level terrain; with approximately 1¼ miles of unavoidable road walking

Starting point: The Crown Inn. The pub does not have a car park but there is some roadside parking available in the village.

How to get there: From Thame take the B4445 Thame to Chinnor road. After approximately 2 miles, turn right along a minor road to Sydenham. The Crown Inn will be on the left.

The **Crown Inn** is a friendly village pub. As you enter you are greeted by a small wooden elephant. The long, low beamed, narrow bar has an open fireplace and a pleasing décor. One wall is adorned with some old photographs of the village, including some of the church, which is situated almost directly opposite the inn. There is a small garden at the rear, with roses in summer. Beers include Greene King IPA and Ruddles County. Soup, baguettes, sausage and mash, duck, salmon and gammon are to be found on the food menu.

Opening times are 12 noon to 2.30 pm and 6 pm to 11 pm on Monday to Saturday; Sunday varies but is usually 12 noon to 3.30 pm and 7 pm to 10.30 pm. Food is available at variable times during the week – it is advisable to ring in advance.

Telephone: 01844 351634.

The Walk

1 With your back to the Crown Inn, cross the road and turn right. In 40 yards, turn left into Brookstones. Pass the Old School Room on your left (don't forget to look out for the plaque) and in 100 yards turn right along an enclosed path, which runs between houses. Go over a stile and bear left to reach a field corner. Turn right across the field to a stile, beside a telegraph pole. Cross the next field, heading just to the left of a cottage. There is a drive just over on your right. At the far side, go through a gap in the hedge and straight across the cottage garden. Cross a stile in the garden fence and bear slightly right over a field to reach a gate and stile. Continue ahead along the right-hand edge of two large fields. Just before the far corner of the second field, turn right over a stile and immediately turn left along the field edge. At the field corner, turn right and at the next corner, bear left over a footbridge and cross the field beyond to reach a road (B4445).

2 Cross, with care, and go over a grassy strip to reach a side road. Turn left and at the road junction swing right along the road signed 'Towersey 1'. Remain on this road until you reach a railway bridge crossing overhead.

3 Immediately after passing under the bridge, turn left between some wooden posts and follow the path up to the disused railway line. This is now a 'Sustrans' cycle route called the 'Phoenix Trail'. Passing a rather modern style seated sculpture, remain on the 'Trail' until you reach a road. Cross the road, with care, and continue along the track opposite. Pass under a road bridge and

continue ahead until you reach an old railway platform. At the far end of the platform, do not go under the road bridge, but turn left, doubling back onto the platform. Now, turn right and follow a narrow metalled path bending right and ascending up to a road. The Falcon pub is on the opposite side of the road to your right.

4 *If you wish to visit Thame, turn right and follow the road into the centre of the town. Return to this point and carry on along the B4012 to continue the walk.*

If you do not intend visiting the town, turn left along the B4012, passing Wenman Road on the left. The B4012 can be quite busy and it is advisable that you use the grass verges as and when they exist. The road crosses over a small stream and starts to ascend gradually. Pass the private gated entrance to Thame Park on the left and in 150 yards look for a footpath sign, also on the left, reading 'Sydenham 2'.

5 Turn left through a gap in the hedge, over a stile, then bear right to a gate leading into Thame Park. Maintain direction across the parkland, following a line of well spread out marker posts. When you are parallel with Thame Park, the house seen on your left, go straight over a drive, and continue ahead to reach a stile and footbridge. Cross these and bear left along the left-hand edge of a field, with a new plantation to your left, to reach a gate and footbridge in the field corner. After crossing the bridge, bear diagonally right across New Park, again following a line of marker posts. There is a good view of the Chiltern Hills from here. At the far corner, go over a stile and

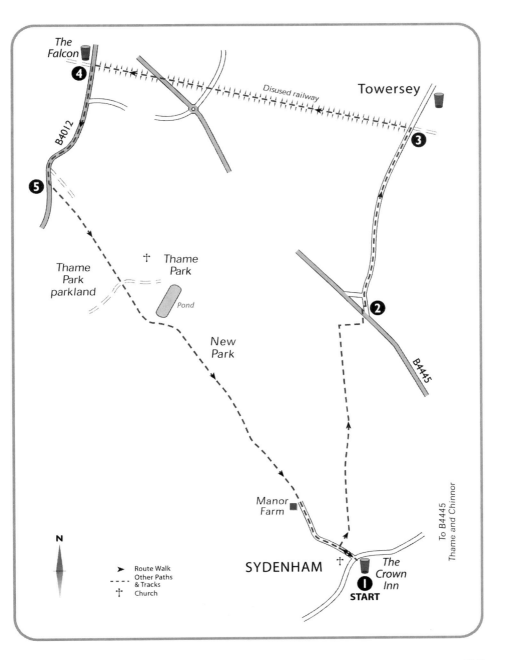

The Falcon

Towersey

Disused railway

B4012

❹

❸

❺

Thame Park parkland

† Thame Park

Pond

New Park

B4445

❷

Manor Farm

SYDENHAM

†

The Crown Inn

❶

START

To B4445
Thame and Chinnor

N

➤ Route Walk
- - - Other Paths
      & Tracks
† Church

An intriguing sculpture-cum-bench on the Phoenix Trail

along the right-hand side of a field. Go over another stile and bear right down a farm track. Ahead, to the right, is the distant radio mast at Stokenchurch. At the bottom go over a stile, just to the left of a gate, and with the entrance to a house called Tays on your right, turn left along a metalled track. Pass to the right of some barns, over a cattle grid, and continue ahead along the lane, passing Manor Farm and the Old School Room, both on your right. At the T-junction, turn right to return to the Crown Inn, which will be just opposite.

Date walk completed:

....

Places of Interest

Sydenham Old School Room was originally built in 1849 when Baroness Wenman, who owned Thame Park at the time, donated land and money for the building. The school, which catered for the education of the village children, was enlarged in 1886. It closed in 1949 and the building is now used as the village hall.

Thame became an important market town in the 13th century. Its importance as a commercial centre resulted in the wide streets we see today. A number of its old inns and houses date back to the 16th century, but the overall façade is mainly Georgian. One well-known coaching inn, the Spread Eagle, is as popular today as it was years ago. Thame Park, the house passed on the walk, is built on the site of a 12th century Cistercian abbey.

The Blue Boar

This super walk starts in Longworth, birthplace of R.D. Blackmore, the author of *Lorna Doone*, and John Fell, who became Dean of Christ Church, Oxford in the 17th century. Leaving the village the route passes Longworth Manor as it heads for Hinton Waldrist, where a window in St Margaret of Antioch's church is dedicated to the late MP Airey Neave who once lived in the village. From there a stretch of country road brings you to Duxford where we join the River Thames at Duxford Ford. After following a 2 mile stroll alongside the tranquil Thames, the route returns to Longworth, via Harrowdown Hill.

The **Blue Boar** was once a bakery and an Elizabethan alehouse. This thatched inn has also featured in a television series called *Private Shultz*. The ceiling of the main bar is adorned with a collection of wooden skis. On the walls can be found a caricature series of 'Men of the Day' and horse racing scenes. The furnishings and dining tables are wooden and there is a settle beside one of the two fireplaces. Beers include Greene King Triumph and Ruddles Best. A good selection of food is available and there is both a lunchtime and evening board to choose from.

Opening times are 12 noon to 3 pm and 6 pm to 11.30 pm on Monday to Saturday and 12 noon to 11 pm on Sunday, if it is busy. Food is available from 12 noon to 2 pm and 7 pm to 9 pm on Monday to Friday; 12 noon to 2.30 pm and 7 pm to 10 pm at weekends (9.30 pm on a Sunday).

Telephone: 01865 820494.

Distance: *5½ miles*

*OS Explorer 170 Abingdon, Wantage & Vale of White Horse and 180 Oxford, Witney & Woodstock
GR 389994*

A mainly level walk with a couple of gentle ascents and descents

Starting point: The Blue Boar. Please obtain permission if you want to use the pub car park while you walk. Some roadside parking is available elsewhere in the village.

How to get there: Turn northwards off the A420 between Oxford and Faringdon, just west of the turning to Kingston Bagpuize, on the road signed to Longworth. The inn is in Tucks Lane in the centre of the village.

The Walk

1 With your back to the Blue Boar turn left along Tucks Lane to the village square. The house on the left, recognised by the post box in the wall, was once the village post office and stores. Turn right along the High Street and at the T-junction turn right again along Church Lane. Just before reaching the church veer left through the entrance drive of Longworth Manor and walk on past a small pond and the manor house itself. Follow the boundary wall round to the right then turn left along an enclosed path. Approaching Hinton Waldrist there is a wonderful panoramic view looking across the Thames Valley to your right. On reaching a road, at a bend and with Glebe Farm over to your left, continue

straight ahead to reach a road junction.

2 Turn right here, passing St Margaret of Antioch's church and Hinton Manor, both on the left. The ¾ mile stretch of road to Duxford is not unpleasant and as you start the descent from Hinton Waldrist there are still good views to be seen. Shortly after passing Dairy Farm on the right the road bends to the left.

3 At the bend, just before a quaint thatched house, turn right at a bridleway sign. Continue ahead past a second thatched house and follow a narrow enclosed path that brings you to Duxford Ford and the River Thames, still in its infancy. Why not have a paddle (weather permitting) before continuing the walk?

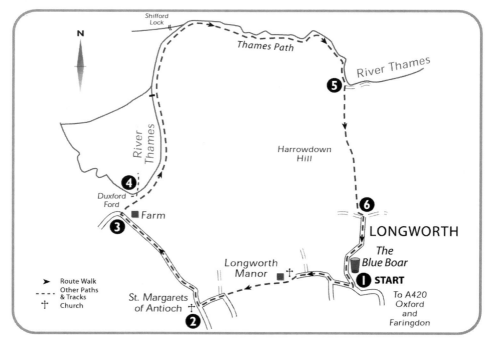

4 Do not cross the ford but turn right up some steps to join a path that runs alongside the river. The route now follows the River Thames for over 2 miles. Staying fairly close to the river the path enters a tunnel of trees and goes through undergrowth before emerging into open fields on the right. The Thames is not easily seen at this

Duxford ford – just the place for a paddle on a hot day

point due to the nettles and reeds that grow between the path and the river. Soon you arrive at, and pass, a new footbridge over the Thames on the left. At this point the route joins the Thames Path. Once the reeds and nettles give way, an enjoyable meandering section of the river is fully open to view the ducks and swans that frequent this area. A couple of stiles are crossed and, at a line of willow trees, go through a swing gate. Continue ahead, with the Thames still on the left, towards a bridge and footpath sign.

5 Just before reaching the footpath sign, veer right across the field to a swing gate at the edge of a copse. Go through the gate, over an arched stone bridge, and follow a path up through the copse. At the top continue along the field edge, heading towards Harrowdown Hill. Go straight over a cross track and ahead on an enclosed track, gradually ascending the hill. There are some fine views to your left. After reaching the top, the track descends to reach a T-junction.

6 Turn left. In 30 yards turn right along a minor road. Level at first, it starts to ascend more steeply as it nears Longworth. The road swings right, then left, passing Glebe Cottage on the left. Ignore a footpath on the right and keep on the road to return to the ivy-covered Blue Boar inn.

Place of Interest
Kingston Bagpuize House and Garden is situated on the A415, just south of the A420 Oxford to Faringdon road. It is an attractive manor house, with a cantilevered staircase and panelled rooms. The garden contains a collection of unusual trees, shrubs and flowers. It is open between 2 pm and 5.30 pm on specific dates between February and October each year. Telephone: 01865 820259.

Date walk completed:

....

The Radnor Arms

Coleshill, a National Trust village overlooking the River Cole, which forms the boundary between Oxfordshire and Wiltshire, is an ideal starting point for this interesting countryside walk. The first part of the circuit takes you, via fields and woods, to Badbury Hill, the site of an Iron Age hill fort. With some magnificent views, the route drops down to Great Coxwell passing the Great Barn, one of the largest medieval tithe barns in the country. The return route takes you through Coleshill Park, which once had a grand 17th century house. It was destroyed by fire in 1952.

The **Radnor Arms** is a typical country pub. Up until 1949 it was the village smithy as indicated on the outside wall. Many of the implements adorning the walls of one of the bars are mementoes of that era. Cosy and snug, it exudes a pleasant and friendly atmosphere. The food menu ranges from sandwiches through to cod, chicken, gammon and steak meals. As to the beer, the inn has a policy of changing its ales on a regular basis.

Opening times are 11 am to 3 pm and 6 pm to 11 pm on Monday to Saturday; 12 noon to 3 pm and 7 pm to 10.30 pm on Sunday. Food is served from 12 noon to 2 pm on Tuesday to Sunday and from 7 pm to 9 pm Tuesday to Saturday (no food on Sunday evening or at any time on a Monday).

Telephone: 01793 861575.

Distance: 6 miles

OS Explorer 170 Abingdon, Wantage & Vale of White Horse
GR 237938

A moderate walk through undulating countryside

Starting point: The Radnor Arms. Please obtain permission if you want to use the pub car park while you walk. Some roadside parking is available in the lay-by opposite the inn.

How to get there: Coleshill is on the B4019 road between Faringdon and Highworth. Heading west, Badbury Hill is about 1½ miles from Faringdon, with Coleshill and the Radnor Arms another 1½ miles further on.

The Walk

1 With your back to the Radnor Arms, turn left and almost immediately turn left again along a narrow lane. At the road junction, cross diagonally left to a footpath sign just opposite. Follow the direction of the sign, going through a gap in the hedge and up the left-hand edge of a field. As you ascend, note the panoramic views to your left. Maintain direction along the edge of a second field and at the far corner drop down to a path taking you through a copse. Where the path bends right, go straight ahead to cross a footbridge and stile. Continue along the edge of the next field, over a stile and along an enclosed path. Go over another footbridge and stile and turn left. At the field corner turn right and in 30 yards, just past a telegraph post, turn left over a footbridge and a stile in the hedge. Bear right across the next field towards Brimstone Farm. Go over a stile and through some scrub to reach a farm track.

2 Turn right, passing to the right of the farm buildings. Cross a concrete lane, go through a gate opposite, and head along the left-hand edge of a field. Go over a footbridge in the far corner and turn left. In 25 yards turn right up the field, with a hedge on your left. Enter Coxwell Wood and follow a narrow path, which ascends gently at first. Go over a cross track and continue uphill ignoring all paths going off left and right. The main path gradually levels out and bends right then left,

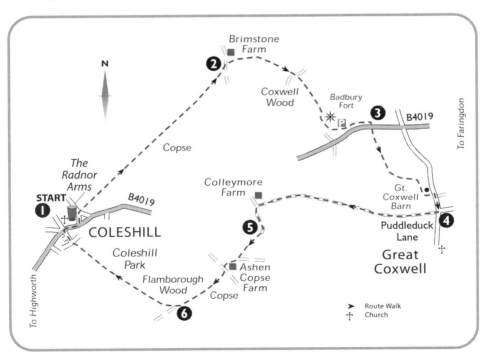

The Great Barn at Coxwell

passing a secluded house on the left, before reaching Badbury Hill National Trust car park. The ramparts of the Iron Age fort are on your left. Go through the car park and, just before reaching the road (B4019), go over a stile on the left. Turn right and follow the field edge, walking parallel with the road.

3 In 250 yards turn right through a gap in the hedge. Cross the road and go through a gate directly opposite. With extensive views of the downs to the south, follow a wide track down the field keeping to the right of a small wood. Just before the bottom corner, turn left over a stile. Follow a path cutting through the corner of the wood to reach another

stile. Cross and turn left along the field edge, following it round as it bends right. The Great Coxwell Barn is now on your left. Cross a stile on the left to visit the barn and reach a road. Turn right along the road to reach a staggered crossroads. (*If you wish to visit the 13th century church of St Giles, from where there are some fine panoramic views to the south, continue ahead at the crossroads, then return to this point.*)

4 Turn right into Puddleduck Lane. Note that one of the cottages on the left is called 'Jemima'. The lane passes some barns on the left and soon becomes a hedged track. When the hedges end, continue ahead across a pasture. Go through a gate and, with a hedge on the right, continue along the next field. At the far corner, ignore a gate on the right and go through the one directly ahead of you. Now turn left along a hedged track to reach a house on the left.

5 Just beyond the house, turn right through a gate and follow the field edge, with a hedge on your right. Go over a stile in the far corner and maintain direction along the edge of the next field. Just before reaching a barn turn right over a stile then turn left to pass to the right of Ashen Copse Farm buildings to join a concrete farm track. Cross over a lane and go through the gate opposite. Follow a clear track, passing a copse on the left and a wood on your right.

6 At the far end of the wood turn right. Follow a path that veers left away from the wood towards a small clump of trees. Maintain direction to reach and go over another stile. Using the distant spire of Coleshill church as a guide, follow an indistinct path across the fields of the Coleshill Estate. At the far side, go through a gate and along a short walled track to reach a road junction. Continue straight ahead to reach the B4019, with Coleshill church directly opposite. Turn right along the pavement to return to the Radnor Arms.

Date walk completed:

....

Places of Interest

The ramparts of **Badbury Hill Fort** are thought to be over 2,500 years old. The site is maintained by the National Trust and can be visited at any time.

Great Coxwell Barn: Cistercian monks from Beaulieu Abbey constructed this great tithe barn in the 13th century. The barn, 150 feet long and 50 feet wide, is built in the shape of a cross. It was used by the monks to store crops and now belongs to the nearby Coleshill Estate, which like the hill fort is the care of the National Trust.

The Swan

Orwell. The walk heads north over Sutton Bridge, passing to the east of Culham and continuing in the direction of the Culham Research Centre. A short stretch alongside the main Didcot to Oxford railway line brings you to the River Thames, which is then followed to Abingdon Bridge. The route

I n the churchyard of All Saints' church, near the start of this walk, you will find the graves of Herbert Henry Asquith, who was Liberal Prime Minister between 1908 and 1916, and Eric Arthur Blair, who was better known as George

returns to Sutton Courtenay alongside the Thames and the Culham Cut.

The **Swan** is an attractive red brick building commanding a prominent position overlooking the village green. On entering via the front porch the main bar is directly ahead of you, while side areas provide appropriate places where you can eat and drink in comfort. Alternatively you can sit outside in a spacious garden. Ales served include Greene King IPA and Morland Original. Sandwiches, ploughman's, lasagne and soup are all available at lunchtime, with more substantial fare on offer in the evening.

Distance: 6¼ miles (add an extra 1 mile if you visit Abingdon)

OS Explorer 170 Abingdon, Wantage & Vale of White Horse
GR 504941

An easy walk on fairly level ground

Starting point: The Swan. Please obtain permission if you want to use the pub car park while you walk. There is very limited parking near the church and near the abbey.

How to get there: Turn off the A415 just south-east of Abingdon, going south through Culham, signposted to Sutton Courtenay. After crossing the Thames, turn right to reach the village green. The Swan is on the left, overlooking the green, just beyond the church.

Opening times are 11.30 am to 2.30 pm and 6 pm to 11 pm on Monday to Saturday; 12 noon to 3 pm and 7 pm to 10.30 pm on Sunday. Food is available from 12 noon to 2 pm every day and from 6 pm to 9 pm on Monday to Saturday; 7 pm to 9 pm on Sunday.

Telephone: 01235 847446.

The Walk

1 Facing the Swan, turn left along the service road. At the corner of All Saints' churchyard wall, turn right along an enclosed path. Pass through a metal barrier and continue ahead to the far end of the churchyard wall where you meet a cross track. (*If you wish to visit the graves of Asquith and Orwell go through the gate on the left just after passing through the barrier. Asquith lies almost directly ahead of you to the right. The headstone of George Orwell is further*

round to the right and reflects his actual name: Eric Arthur Blair).

2 Turn left along All Saint's Lane to reach a road, with the Fish pub on the corner. Cross the road and go along the private road opposite (signed 'Thames Path ½'). Where the private road ends go over a stile and ahead along the left-hand edge of a field. Ignore stiles to your left as these lead to private fishing areas. Soon you have a stream on your left. Where the field narrows bear right to go through a swing gate. Turn left along the

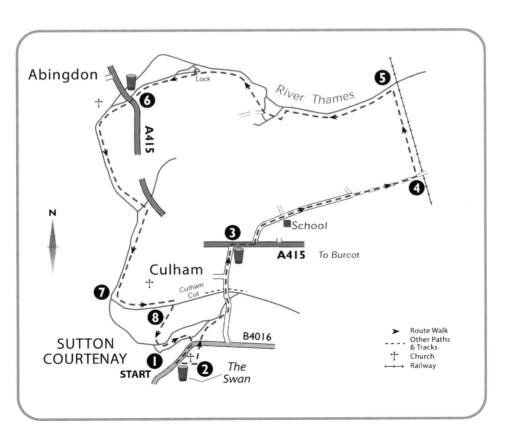

Abingdon Bridge

road over Sutton Bridge. As you cross Culham Cut Bridge note Culham Lock down to your left. You may be lucky enough to see some river craft going through. Ignoring all turnings left and right continue along the road until you reach a road junction (A415), with the Waggon and Horses pub on the right.

❸ Cross the road with care, using the traffic island, and turn right. In 300 yards, at a road sign indicating 'European School', turn left into Thame Lane. After passing the school, on your right, the road narrows. Over to your left on a distant hilltop you can see Wittenham Clumps. Where the road turns left to Warren Farm House continue straight ahead along a rough track.

❹ Where the track crosses over the Didcot to Oxford railway line, turn left along an enclosed path that runs parallel with the line. The path alternates with the field edge and drops down, passing a motorcycle-scrambling course to your left.

❺ At the bottom corner of the field, turn left. Keeping to the field edge, the River Thames soon becomes visible on your right. At the far end of the second field the path swings left then right to cross two bridges over a stream. After crossing the second bridge there is a display board that provides information about the first Thames Pound Lock that once existed at this point. The path veers right and rejoins the bank of the Thames, which is then followed to Abingdon Lock. Do not cross the lock but continue ahead to reach Abingdon Bridge.

6 *To visit Abingdon, go up the steps to your left and turn right over Abingdon Bridge, passing the Nags Head pub on your way to the town centre.*

To continue the walk, go straight ahead under the bridge, through parkland. After passing Abingdon church, on the opposite side of the Thames, a pleasant stretch of the river is followed. The stacks of Didcot Power Station, creating an imposing sight, can be seen directly ahead of you. After crossing over a wooden bridge bear right to continue along the Thames Path until you reach the western end of the Culham Cut.

7 The path swings left here along the bank of the Cut. In 600 yards you reach a bridge on your right where a sign indicates 'Sutton Courtenay ½ mile'.

8 Turn right over the bridge and bear right across fields to reach a bridge over the Thames. The path bears left and crosses a number of bridges and weirs. At the far end turn right over a bridge, boarded on the left, through a gate, then ahead to reach a road. Cross the road and turn right past some delightful old wood-beam houses on the left to reach the George and Dragon pub and the village green. Bear left to return to the Swan.

> **Date walk completed:**
>
> ....

Places of Interest

Abingdon was, until 1867, the county town of Berkshire – today it is in Oxfordshire. The County Hall, described as one of the finest in England, is well worth seeing. Christopher Kempster, who worked on St Paul's with Sir Christopher Wren, built it in the late 17th century. Abingdon Bridge is a listed structure.

Didcot Railway Centre, situated near Didcot Railway Station, south of Sutton Courtenay, is open on Saturdays and Sundays throughout the year and daily at various periods between April and October. As these periods tend to change it is worth checking before setting out to relive the golden age of steam and the Great Western Railway. Telephone: 01235 817200.

The Carriers Arms

This interesting walk, starting from Watlington, takes in sections of two of the long distance paths that run through Oxfordshire – the Ridgeway and the Oxfordshire Way. A fairly steep ascent brings you to Christmas Common

Distance: *6 miles*

OS Explorer 171 Chiltern Hills West
GR 692944

A moderate walk with one fairly steep ascent and one gradual descent

Starting point: The Carriers Arms. Please obtain permission if you want to use the pub car park while you walk. Parking is also available in the public car park in Hill Road, closer to the town.

How to get there: Leave the M40 at junction 6 and take the B4009 south-east, signed to Watlington. As you enter the town turn left into Hill Road. The Carriers Arms is on the left just beyond the public car park on the right.

and Watlington Hill, from where you will have some excellent views to the north. A short detour off route takes you to the viewpoint. The hill has a large white (chalk) scar carved into the hillside; best seen from the pub car park. The route descends to join the Ridgeway, which is followed for a short distance before returning to Watlington.

The **Carriers Arms**, being close to the Ridgeway and the local farming community, contains a number of old cartwheels adorning the low ceiling bars. The floor is carpeted and most of the seats are fabric covered. Beside one of the bars is a framed verse entitled *The Man Behind the Bar*. A good choice of food is available, ranging from breakfasts and including sandwiches as well as something more substantial. Beer includes Adnams, Bass and Loddon Hoppit. On fine days you can sit in the garden, where children and dogs are welcome, and enjoy the view of Watlington Hill and the Chiltern escarpment. You may even see a kite or two. Alternatively you can play 'Aunt Sally'.

Opening times are 9 am to 11 pm on Monday to Saturday; 9 am to 3 pm and 7 pm to 11 pm on Sunday. Food is available from 9 am until 2 pm (Sunday until 3 pm) for breakfasts and lunch and from 7 pm to 9.30 pm every day.

Telephone: 01491 613470.

The Walk

1 Leave the Carriers Arms car park and turn left up Hill Road. Pass Watlington Hospital and the entrance to a Camping and Caravan Club site on the right and in a further 75 yards, where the road starts to rise steeply, you reach a cross track (the Ridgeway).

2 Turn left and follow the heavily rutted track for ¾ mile, to where a minor road crosses it.

3 Here, turn right along the Oxfordshire Way. The tree-covered Pyrton Hill can be seen ahead to your left. Ignoring a gate and path on your left, continue along the metalled road, passing Pyrton Hill House

on the right. When the metalled surface ends, continue up a grassy track. Where this bends right go straight ahead across the grass. Pass to the right of a telegraph post with a white arrow on it, and follow a meandering path as it ascends quite steeply up Aston Hill. Near the top, the path widens. Look out for a stile on the right with a painted sign on it stating 'PY1'. Fork right to go over a stile and up a bank into a field. Follow the right-hand edge of the field. Ignore a stile on the right and continue along the field edge to reach a stile and road.

4 Turn right and at the first road junction turn right, signed to Watlington. Follow the road for 440 yards until you see the corner of a

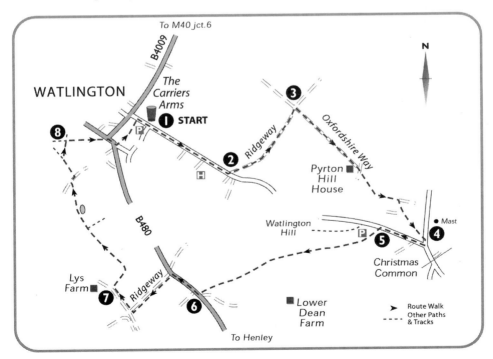

National Trust car park on the left. (*To visit Watlington Hill, go through the car park to the far left-hand corner where there is a path leading to the viewpoint at the top of the hill. The views are well worth this short detour. To continue the walk, return to point 5, where you turn right.*)

5 Turn left along an enclosed path (W7) going through an avenue of trees. Continue along the path, through a swing gate and almost immediately fork right (note the white arrow on a tree). The path descends gradually through trees to reach another swing gate. Still descending, views begin to open up ahead to your left. Lower Dean, the farm snuggling in the valley to your left, also comes into view. As the path levels out, ignore a path joining from the left and continue ahead to reach another swing gate. Ignore a stepped path on the right. Go through the gate and follow a narrow meandering path through a band of trees. Go through a gate, over a farm track, and through another gate before continuing ahead. Pass between two houses and on emerging at a track turn right to reach a road.

6 Turn right for 300 yards to reach our old friend, the Ridgeway (signed 'Dame Alice Farm'). Here, turn left and, almost immediately, turn left again over a stile. Turn right along the field edge. At the far corner go over a stile and turn right to reach a multi-track junction. Bear right across the Ridgeway to a stile to the right of a metalled track. Keep to the left-hand edge of a field to reach another stile in the far corner, near Lys Farm.

7 Go over the stile and turn right across

a yard to join a track running alongside the right-hand edge of a field, with a wire fence on the left. Keep with the wire fence as it bends left and follow an enclosed track running between fields. Ignore a path going right and continue ahead to pass to the left of a small copse and stagnant pond. At a cross track, with a gate to your left, turn right and in a few yards turn left, heading towards some red-roofed houses. In 300 yards turn right along an enclosed path, with a ditch on the right.

8 At a T-junction, turn right to go through a swing gate. Bear left across a field to a gate in the far corner. Go through and along an enclosed path to emerge at a road. Turn right, passing Lilacs Place on the right and a road junction on the left. Just before the road bends sharply to the right, turn left along Watcombe Road. At the far end, turn left, then right to reach Hill Road. Turn right to return to the Carriers Arms, which will be on your left.

Place of Interest

Stonor House and Deer Park is situated 5 miles north of Henley-on-Thames, on the B480 between Henley and Watlington. It has been the historic home of Lord and Lady Camoys and the Stonor family for over 800 years. The house, which contains rare furniture and tapestries, is open from 2 pm to 5.30 pm on Sundays between April and September, on Wednesdays during July and August, and on Bank Holiday Mondays. Telephone: 01491 638587.

Date walk completed:

....

The Fox and Hounds

experience he later captured in his well-loved novel *Tom Brown's Schooldays*. The walk crosses fields, including the line of the old canal, to the village of Fawler, before heading along the valley to Woolstone. The return through Uffington passes 'Tom Brown's School', now a museum, and the 13th century St Mary's church, 'The Cathedral of the Vale', which is well worth a visit.

Uffington, situated in the Vale of the White Horse, was once a thriving agricultural community served by the now disused Wiltshire and Berkshire Canal, which closed in 1910. The author Thomas Hughes attended school here as a young boy, an

Distance: 6 miles

OS Explorer 170 Abingdon, Wantage & Vale of White Horse
GR 306893

This is a fairly level walk, mainly across agricultural land

Starting point: The Memorial Hall car park in Fawler Road.

How to get there: From the B4507 Wantage to Ashbury road turn north along a minor road signed to Uffington. At a junction turn right, passing the Fox and Hounds on the right, and turn right at a T-junction. The Memorial Hall is the first building on the right.

The **Fox and Hounds** in Uffington's High Street, just south of the start/finish of the walk, is a small friendly village pub with a plain décor. The stone-floored bar is divided into two rooms, one has a brick fireplace and the other has an old radio sitting on a shelf above the door and lanterns hanging from the ceiling. The food is simple and straightforward and includes scampi, chicken and ham and eggs as well as a Sunday roast. Children's portions are also available. The main ales come from the West Berkshire Brewery and include Uffington Ale.

Opening times are 11 am to 3 pm on Monday, Wednesday and Thursday – closed on Tuesday lunchtime – and 6 pm to 11 pm on Monday to Thursday; 11 am to 11 pm on Friday and Saturday; 12 noon to 10.30 pm on Sunday. Food is available from 12 noon until 2.30 pm except on Tuesday (Sunday from 12 noon until 4 pm).

Telephone: 01367 820680.

The Walk

1 Leave the Memorial Hall car park, cross the road and turn left. In 40 yards turn right along The Green and at a junction fork right along Lower Common. Just past the last house on the right, go over a stile on the right. Bear left across the field, over two stiles, maintaining direction across a second field to a stile in the far corner. Cross a farm track and a stile opposite then continue in the same direction across the next field to reach a stile, and Fawler Road. Turn left for 150 yards then turn left into Uffington Gorse (there is a Woodland Trust sign on the gate). Follow a narrow path through the wood for 100 yards and, at a junction, turn right to reach a gate and minor road.

2 Turn right to reach the junction with Fawler Road. Cross with care and go through the right-hand gate opposite. With a hedge on your left continue along the field edge for 440 yards to reach a small drainage channel. Continue ahead into the next field and, in 40 yards, bear right across the field, aiming towards a line of trees. At the far side, go over a footbridge and through a narrow belt of trees to reach a broken stile. This narrow belt of trees forms the route of the old Wiltshire and Berkshire Canal. Cross the stile and maintain direction across the next field to reach a stile and road.

3 Turn left into Fawler village. Ignoring a path on the left, continue ahead past Fawler Manor on the left to reach Fawler Cottage, on the right.

4 Just past the cottage, turn right at a

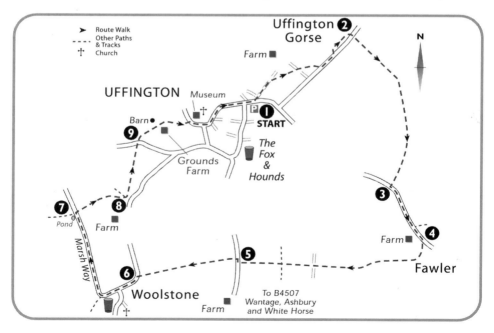

132

footpath sign (Woolstone 1¾). Go through a gate and bear left across the field to a footbridge and gate at the far side. Go through and across the next field, through a small plantation and into the next field. Maintain direction across the next field, aiming towards the right-hand edge of a hedge at the far side. There are good views of White Horse Hill from these fields but the White Horse itself is not visible. Go over a stile, to the right of a gate, and head across the next field towards the far left-hand corner. Go through a gate and maintain direction across two more fields to reach a road. Turn right for 20 yards to a stile on the left, signed 'Woolstone ½'. (*You can shorten the walk at this point by following the road back into Uffington.*)

5 Go over the stile and along the edge of two fields, the first a paddock and the second a small plantation. At the far corner, go ahead through some trees and scrub to cross a stile. Continue ahead along the edge of two fields. White Horse Hill may be visible over to your left between gaps in the hedge.

6 On reaching a road, turn left into Woolstone, passing some attractive cottages on the right. At a road junction go straight ahead. Pass the White Horse Inn on the left and follow the road round a sharp right-hand bend. Carry on along Marsh Way until you reach a small pond on your left. Just beyond it is a footpath sign.

7 Here, turn right over a stile and head across the field, keeping about 20 yards from the right-hand edge. Go over a footbridge at the far side; then turn left along the field edge. Cross a stile and footbridge in the far corner and continue

along a narrow path, which runs between a small ditch and a cottage garden.

8 Just before reaching a road, at a three-way footpath sign, turn left over a stile beside a gate. Keep to the right of a second gate and head across a field to a footbridge, to the right of the far left-hand corner. Cross the bridge then bear left across the field to reach a road.

9 Cross to a path opposite. Bear right across the field, keeping to the left of Grounds Farm. Between a midfield barn and the farm turn right to reach a stile in the hedge of the farm entrance drive. Turn left along the drive to a road. Turn right uphill to a junction, with Tom Brown's School Museum on the left. Turn left, past the church, following the road through the village and back to the Memorial Hall.

Places of Interest

Tom Brown's School Museum is open at weekends and on Bank Holiday Mondays from 2 pm to 5 pm between Easter Saturday and the end of October. Telephone: 01367 820259.

The **White Horse** and **Uffington Castle**, situated to the south of Uffington village, are open at all times. The chalk carving of the White Horse, 365 ft long and 130 ft tall, is thought to be over 3,000 years old. Uffington Castle, an Iron Age hill fort, covers an area of 8 acres. To visit them, take the road south out of Uffington, go over the B4507 and continue up the hill to reach some car parks on the left.

Date walk completed:

East Hendred
The Plough Inn

This enjoyable walk starts in the lovely old village of East Hendred. Steeped in history, its roots date back to an early Saxon settlement. Hendred House, passed on the latter part of the walk, has been in the Eyston family since 1453. The family was related, through marriage, to Sir Thomas More, Chancellor to Henry VIII. Leaving the village, the route crosses fields to West Hendred, then on to Ardington, with its 12th century Holy Trinity church and Ardington House, a 18th century mansion. Returning to East Hendred, the route follows the Icknield Way, from where there are some great views.

Distance: 6 miles

OS Explorer 170 Abingdon, Wantage & Vale of White Horse
GR 459889

A gentle walk through gently undulating countryside, with one very short ascent

Starting point: The Plough Inn. Please obtain permission if you want to use the pub car park while you walk. Limited parking is available elsewhere in the village.

How to get there: East Hendred is situated 4 miles east of Wantage. From the A417 Wantage to Reading road, take a turning south, signed to East Hendred. As you enter the village turn right into Orchard Lane; the Plough will be on your left.

The **Plough Inn**, which dates back to the 16th century, has lofty raftered beams in the main bar and restaurant areas. A plough stands firmly on top of one of the rafters and other agricultural and farm implements adorn the walls. A cartwheel lamp holder hangs from the ceiling. A side bar contains a pool table and television set. A spacious and pleasant garden has an 'Aunt Sally' pitch in one corner. Ales available include Greene King IPA, Morland, and Caledonian 80/-. Baguettes, ciabatta, paninis and jacket potatoes are included on the lunch menu, with more substantial fare, including à la carte and chef's specials, available in the evening. It is advisable to book for Sunday lunch.

Opening times are 12 noon to 3 pm and 6 pm to 11 pm on weekdays; 12 noon to 11 pm on Saturday; 12 noon to 10.30 pm on Sunday. Food is available from 12 noon to 2 pm and 7 pm to 9.30 pm every day except Monday evening.

Telephone: *01235 833213.*

The Walk

1 Leave the inn car park and turn left along Orchard Lane. At the road junction, cross and continue along Mill Lane opposite. Pass Hendred Sports Club and playing fields on the left and at the next cottage turn left onto an enclosed path. The path bends right, passing between the thatched cottage and a bungalow, before dropping down through some trees to cross a footbridge over a stream. Bear left across a field to a stile in a wooden fence gap at a hedge corner. Aim to the right of a nearby farm. Go over and along the left-hand edge of the next field. Cross another stile and walk along a short enclosed section to reach a farm track. Cross this and the stile opposite, and then turn left down a second track to reach a road.

Turn right along the road into West Hendred.

2 At a T-junction, turn right uphill, passing the village notice board. In 200 yards, just past Bankside, turn left onto a path signed 'Ardington 1'. Follow the path across the middle of a large field and at the far side, turn left along a farm track. In 30 yards turn right along the edge of a field, with a wire fence on your left. At the far corner, go through a gap in the hedge. Go over a stile and bear slightly left across the next field. Maintain direction across three further fields, passing through gaps in the hedge lines between each one. At the far side of the third field, go through a gate and along a farm track. The track, which becomes metalled, soon reaches a road junction. Turn right here and follow

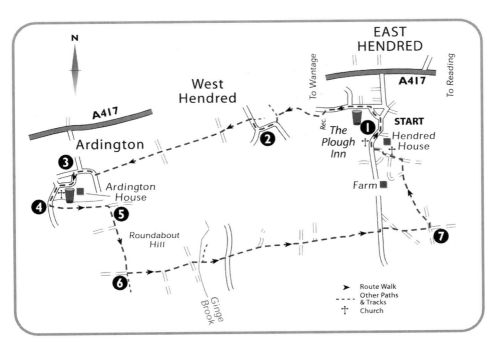

the road round into Ardington. At the next road junction carry straight ahead along High Street.

3 At the next road junction, with Butcher's Yard on the right, turn left into Church Street. The road bends right and you pass the entrance to Ardington House and, soon after, the Boars Head pub and Holy Trinity church. Inside the church there is a statue of a kneeling woman reputed to have been carved by the designer of Nelson's Column. At the road junction, fork to the left of a grassy triangle and follow the road down to cross the bridge over Ardington Brook.

4 Continue up the road for 25 yards, then turn left along a grassy track. In 350 yards, a gap opens up to your left, where you will have a clear view of Ardington House. Views of the downs are seen to your right. Continue along the track until you reach a track junction.

5 Turn right here onto a rough farm track. Gradually ascending, the track passes some farm buildings and the tree-covered Roundabout Hill, both on your left, to reach a cross track at the top of the field. This is an old Roman road called the Icknield Way.

6 Turn left onto the Icknield Way. The route now follows this ancient thoroughfare for the next 1¾ miles. If you have chosen a fine clear day, you will have some wonderful panoramic views. At one point the route crosses a track and descends through trees to cross a bridge over Ginge Brook. The path rises quite steeply up the bank on the far side to reach a field, where it again widens out. Cross over a road and maintain direction

until you reach a second road. Go straight across and continue along the right of way opposite. Where the metalled track veers right, carry straight on, keeping to the left of a dense plantation.

7 Where the plantation ends, turn left. In 30 yards, fork left along a track (Cow Road). Go straight over a cross track and head towards the houses of East Hendred, ignoring a track on the left. The path drops down to meet a cross path. Fork left here to reach a road. Turn right to pass under the arch that connects St Mary's Catholic church with its presbytery. At the next road junction turn right along St Mary's Road and follow it round a left-hand bend to reach another road junction. Turn right to pass St Augustine of Canterbury church on your left. Continue uphill passing the tree-lined entrance to Hendred House on your right, and at the next road junction, fork to the left of the war memorial. Pass the Wheatsheaf pub and continue round a right-hand bend to reach Orchard Lane. Turn left to return to the Plough Inn.

Place of Interest

Wantage, 4 miles to the west of East Hendred, is the birthplace of King Alfred the Great. A statue commemorating this legendary king stands in the Market Square. George Street, the Victorian architect who designed London's Law Courts, was also born here. There are many interesting 17th to 19th century buildings, which give the town its special character.

Date walk completed:

....

The Lamb Inn

Chiltern beech woods, which in spring and autumn are a mass of colour. You also pass Greys Court, a picturesque Tudor style house with an interesting history. The return to Satwell takes in some more delightful Chiltern woods.

The **Lamb Inn** is a traditional country pub. The building was originally a farm worker's cottage and dates back to the 16th century. It has been a public house for more than 200 years and is reputed to be haunted by a ghost called 'George'. The interior consists of a low-beamed main bar with a large fireplace and a separate dining area. Outside there is a small garden. There is a varied and comprehensive choice of meals ranging from salads and baguettes to steak and ale pie and more substantial fare. Real ales include Brakspear Special and seasonal ales such as Bee Sting.

Opening times are 11 am to 3 pm and 6 pm to 11 pm on Monday to Saturday and 12 noon to 10 pm on Sunday. Food is served from 12 noon to 2 pm and 7 pm to 9.30 pm on Monday to Saturday; 12 noon until 6 pm on Sunday.

Telephone: 01491 628482.

T his colourful walk starts from the small village of Satwell, which is situated within the parish of Rotherfield Greys a few miles to the west of Henley on Thames. The route takes you through some of the beautiful

Distance: 5½ miles

OS Explorer 171 Chiltern Hills West GR 706834

A moderate walk with some short ascents and descents

Starting point: The Lamb Inn car park. Please obtain permission if you want to leave your car while you are walking. Parking elsewhere in the village is limited.

How to get there: From Nettlebed on the A4130, take the B481 south for 2½ miles then bear left at a road junction, signed to Shepherd's Green. The Lamb Inn is about 150 yards on the right.

The Walk

1 Leave the pub car park and turn left for 150 yards. Just beyond the road junction look for a stile on the right. Go over and follow a narrow path meandering just inside the wood edge. Go over a cross track and in 40 yards, at the next junction, swing left and follow the path to reach a stile and minor road. Turn right along the road and where the main road swings right continue ahead along the Nettlebed Estate drive.

2 Immediately before some gates and a cattle grid, turn left along a bridleway. Pass a gate and continue ahead along the main track. Ignore a couple of paths going off to the left and in 700 yards you arrive at a cross path recognisable by surrounding rhododendron bushes.

3 Here, turn right along a grassy track. Ignore a path on the right and continue straight ahead. On reaching a stile go over and ahead across a short stretch of field to reach a drive. Turn left over a cattle grid and follow the drive for 600 yards to reach a cross drive. Bromsden Cottages are just on the left.

4 Turn right towards Bromsden Farm. Pass between the farm buildings and a barn and just beyond the barn bear right to join a path leading into the wood. The path bends left, then right, and descends

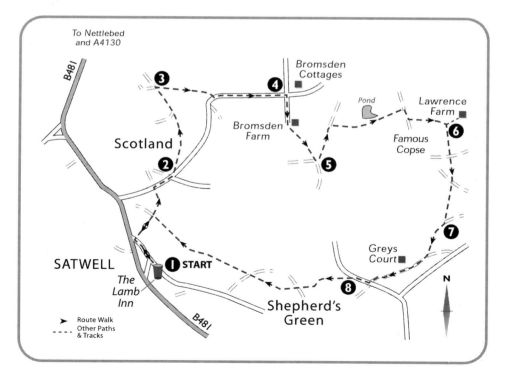

Greys Court

gradually. There is a small wire fence on the right. At the bottom, where a path joins from the right, go ahead for 10 yards to a path junction.

5 Turn left here and, ignoring a path ascending on the right, continue along the valley bottom for 300 yards. Now look for a faint path on the right ascending fairly steeply. Continue uphill until you reach a high bank at the top. Bear right here and follow a path up the bank to reach and go over a stile. Turn left along the field edge, passing to the right of a small pond. Just beyond the pond go over a stile on the left and turn right along the field edge. At a farm track, turn right. Soon bear left to cross a stile at the edge of a wood. In 10 yards turn left over a

second stile and follow a path through Famous Copse.

6 At the far corner, swing right, still keeping inside the wood edge. At a cross track continue ahead, as signed. Go over a second cross path to reach a stile at the field edge. Beyond the stile, take the right-hand path across the field, passing under some telegraph wires. Cross a drive and stile and walk over the field to another stile on the far side. Go down some steps and across the next field. There is a large barn to your left. Go through a gap into the wood and follow a fenced path down to reach and go through a gate.

7 Go down a few steps and turn right along a fenced path. Walk over a wooden platform and in 30 yards turn left over a stile. Turn right along the field edge, going through a gate and up across a field and car park to reach a metalled drive. Turn right past a kiosk and keep to the drive as it passes to the left of Greys Court. At a junction bear left downhill. Where the drive bends left to a road go straight ahead across the grass to cross a stile in the corner and out to the road. Ignoring a stile opposite, turn right along the road for 200 yards to reach a stile on the left.

8 Go over the stile and walk up the right-hand edge of a field. Cross another stile into a wood and ascend steeply through the trees to a path junction. Bear right over a stile and at the next junction fork right. Go over a cross track and at a T-junction bear right to reach the wood edge. Walk along a narrow enclosed path, then along a field edge to emerge at a junction of drives. Go ahead

for 20 yards before turning right to pass a small thatched cottage on your right. Where the drive bends right continue ahead along a grassy track, bending right to reach a gate and stile (footpath sign). Go over the stile and immediately turn left along the field edge. Cross another stile and bear right across the next field to the wood corner. Keep ahead with the wood on your left and at the next wood corner go over a stile, a track and a stile opposite. Maintain direction across two fields to reach the edge of a wood. Enter the wood and in 40 yards, at a cross path, turn left and follow the path through the wood to reach a stile and road. Turn left and retrace your steps back to the Lamb Inn.

Date walk completed:

....

Place of Interest

Greys Court is an intriguing and picturesque Tudor style house with an attractive courtyard. Although looked after by the National Trust, it has been in the Brunner family since the 1930s. The house and garden are open at specific times between March and September. Times should be checked before visiting. Telephone: 01491 628529.

This interesting walk starts at the small village of Shiplake Row situated on the hillside north of the River Thames. The route takes in Shiplake church where the poet Alfred Lord Tennyson was married in 1850. Behind the church are the interesting buildings of Shiplake College. A riverside walk along the bank of the Thames brings you to Sonning, with its fascinating Mill Theatre and Restaurant. From there the route takes in road, path and track on its return to Shiplake Row.

The White Hart has three connecting rooms used as two bars and a dining area. There is also a pleasant garden at the rear where dogs are welcome. The inn has a relaxed and friendly atmosphere throughout. Soup, sandwiches and ploughman's are all on the menu, as well as chicken curry and more substantial fare. Children's portions are also available. Real ales include Brakspear Special.

Distance: 6½ miles

OS Explorer 171 Chiltern Hills West GR 756785

A mainly level walk with one gradual ascent

Starting point: The White Hart car park. Please obtain permission if you want to leave your car while you walk. There is extra parking at the Scout Hut further up the road if not in use.

How to get there: At Shiplake take a minor road west off the A4155 Henley to Reading road, signed to Binfield Heath. The White Hart will be on the left.

Opening times are 12 noon to 3 pm and 6 pm to 11 pm on Monday to Saturday; 12 noon to 3 pm and 7 pm to 10.30 pm on Sunday. Food is served at lunchtime from 12 noon to 2 pm every day; in the evening from 6.30 pm to 9 pm on Monday to Saturday and from 7 pm to 9 pm on Sunday.

Telephone: 0118 940 3673.

The Walk

1 With your back to the pub turn right. Just beyond the car park turn right along the edge of a field, with the boundary hedge of the White Hart on your right. When the hedge ends bear slightly left across the field, aiming towards a telegraph post. There are good views of the Thames Valley ahead. On reaching a cross path turn left and at the field corner turn right. In 300 yards turn left over a stile (note the faded footpath sign) and continue along the field edge towards the houses of Shiplake. With Shiplake Court Farm on your right, go through a swing gate and ahead along a farm track to reach a road.

2 Turn right, passing Plowden Way on the left, and follow the road to its junction with the A4155. The Plowden Arms is on your right. Cross the A4155 diagonally left to Church Lane opposite. The signpost reads 'Shiplake Church – 12th C – medieval glass – Lord Tennyson married here 1850'. Follow the lane to the church. The buildings of Shiplake College are just behind it. Where the church wall ends bear right down a stepped path to reach the corner of a farm road. Here, turn left along a gravelled track to reach the River Thames. Shiplake College Clubroom is just on your right.

3 Skirt around the clubroom building,

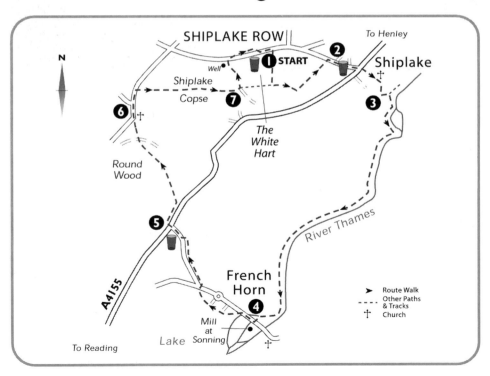

Shiplake church where Alfred Lord Tennyson was married

keeping the Thames on your left, and go over a wooden footbridge. The route now follows the Thames Path to Sonning Bridge. This is a very pleasant part of the walk, watching the various types of river craft passing by as they journey both up and down stream. As you near Sonning Bridge the path crosses a footbridge over the side stream that once fed the old Sonning Mill and emerges at a road. The entrance to the mill, now a dining theatre, is directly opposite.

4 Turn right along the road, over Backwater Bridge, to reach the French Horn Hotel. Now cross the road, with care, and keep to the left of the hotel car park. At Furleigh Cottages bear right along an enclosed path. At a minor road, turn left and follow the road as it bends right past a thatched barn. At the next road junction continue ahead, passing the entrance to Reading Sailing Club on the left. At the far end, go through a gate and cross the road. Go through another gate, to the right of the minor road opposite. Keep to the left-hand edge of an allotment, then a couple of fields. Just before the far corner of the second field go through a gate on the left and turn right along the road to reach a road junction (A4155). The Flowing Spring pub is just on your left.

5 Cross the road with care. Pass between the railings opposite, go up a few steps and then turn right along the field edge. Just 30 yards before the field corner turn right through a gap in the hedge, then turn left along part of an old road. In 30 yards, fork left up an enclosed path. Go straight over a cross track and continue along a narrow path. At the far end the path widens to a gravel drive before reaching a road.

6 Turn right. Pass Binfield Heath Congregational church with its mini square tower and, 30 yards after passing the 'Old Club House', turn right at a footpath sign – Shiplake 1½. Follow the path along the edge of two fields and at the far corner go over a stile and into Shiplake Copse – a good place for bluebells in springtime. At the bottom, ignore a path going off right and bear left over a stile at the wood edge. It can get very wet here due to springs. Continue ahead up the left-hand edge of a field. Where the hedge bends left go straight ahead across the open field to pick up the field edge again in 50 yards. At the far side, go through a gap in the hedge to reach a cross path.

7 Turn left along a path lined by trees and hedges until you reach a road. Note the cupola-topped brick well at the roadside. 'Keeps Well', which was established by Admiral Swinburne, supplied water for the village during the late 1800s. Turn right along the road and in 150 yards, at Shiplake Rise Farm, cross the road to a footpath running parallel to the road on the opposite side. Just before a private area bear right down some steps to the road and turn left to return to the White Hart, which will be on your right.

Place of Interest
The River & Rowing Museum, situated at Mill Meadows in Henley on Thames provides a unique interpretation of the Thames from its source to the Thames Barrier. It also includes an engrossing history of Britain's rowing heritage. The museum has a full programme of special exhibitions. Telephone: 01491 415600.

Date walk completed:

....